BODY PARTS

and the

Invisible You

John Murray

ISBN: 978-1-77084-990-7

10   9   8   7   6   5   4

Publication assistance by

PAGEMASTER
PUBLISHING
PageMaster.ca

Contents

To friends I know and have known,
who have supported and encouraged me
on this journey of life.

Introduction

What is it that makes us tick? Why does each of us react to situations differently? Why do we think the way we do? Is mind over matter a reality? Are you ever amazed at human endeavors? Are we living to make a difference? Do we work for change? Are we making a positive contribution to our society?

These are questions that make us take stock of ourselves and check the result of our actions. We need to reflect on life, or we may find ourselves living in a cruise-control mode. Life itself should make us think.

How much do you think about the past? Do you look back at the road you have traveled? Do you ever consider what has happened to you and how you have been brought to where you are today? How has your past affected you? How has it affected others around you? Could you have reacted differently in some areas? Should you have acted differently? Should you have responded instead of reacting?

Following is a collection of pieces, some of which were originally written for social media, but have been revised and re-written. Others are new. The subjects are as varied as life itself, covering common and not-so-common issues. They have been inspired by things I have read, by events that have taken place, or things people have said. When the subjects came to my attention they made my little grey cells work overtime and eventually resulted in putting pen to paper—well at least type to screen.

Some chapters you might find humorous, others perhaps more serious, and who knows, maybe you'll even shed a tear or two. You will not agree with everything, and that is how it should be. We are all different, have our own opinions, and see things from a different perspective. These chapters simply convey life as I have experienced it.

I trust you will find some of the subjects encouraging, uplifting, and even challenging, but I hope you find all of them to be somewhat thought provoking. If just one chapter brings you comfort or lifts you up to a higher plane and makes your day brighter, then my efforts will have been worthwhile.

I.

Can We Talk Body Parts?

The transplanting of human organs has now developed into a massive worldwide operation. Sadly, it has even birthed a black market. People are willing to pay huge sums of money for body parts which are available immediately. Refugees have been discovered selling kidneys for thousands of dollars to fund their escape to the West. Regrettably, some lose a kidney and their money to unscrupulous thugs.

On the positive side the parents of a young boy killed in a car accident donated his organs to various recipients. His heart went on beating for another 21 years in the chest of an older man. The cornea of his eyes gave sight to two other people. His kidneys brought relief to other patients suffering with renal problems. It was delightful to see a photo of the parents and all the people who had a better life health-wise because of their kind action through their son.

Prosthetic arms and legs have been commonplace since most of us can remember. In fact, as early as 2500 BC there is a reference in Egyptian writings to a queen Vishpala having an iron prosthesis to replace a leg she lost in battle. The Greeks were also into making artificial limbs. However, we are here considering the transplantation of live body organs. In the last 50 to 60 years we have seen heart, kidney, and liver transplants. We have seen more than one full-face transplant. Even a double hand transplant has been successfully accomplished.

Another organ transplanted is now the penis. During 2016, it was announced that a man had successfully fathered a child after having a penis transplant. Apparently, there is a huge demand for this in Africa, where many men suffer from the results of botched circumcision operations.

We might think, "Where will they go from here?" Well, it would appear that no organ or part of the body is beyond consideration. Medical scientists indicate that it is now possible to transplant a complete head! Think about that for a moment. If you will excuse the pun, it is mind-blowing!

Apparently, they have already tried it with three monkeys—poor monkeys. Two lasted a matter of hours, with no movement below the neck. The other one had partial movement below the neck but died after eleven days.

Can you imagine being asked if you would like a new head? I asked my wife, if she had an inoperable brain tumor, would she like a new head. She definitively replied, "No, thank you!" How would you know what was already in that head? I am not sure the head would arrive empty like a computer that had the memory wiped clean.

We might think it outlandish, but reportedly a Russian gentleman named Valeri Spiridonov, who suffers from a "muscle wasting disease," is willing to have his head transplanted to a donor body. There is also an Italian surgeon, Sergio Canavero, willing to undertake the operation. It is planned for December 2017. In fact, by the time you read this it may have occurred, although I suspect it was cancelled or postponed. Just my doubts rising to the surface.

Those surgeons who experimented with the monkeys estimate that the operation on a human being would need 80 surgeons, with many other medical personnel, and could take 36 hours or more to complete. The cost would be in the multiple millions of dollars. I have an idea that it will not become too common.

My question would be, "Is the body receiving a new head or is the head receiving a new body?" I conclude it is the latter. If you had your head lopped off and replaced with another, who would continue to live? It wouldn't be you but the person in the new head.

All things considered, it would be a body transplant and not a head transplant. If your body was incapacitated and likely to worsen, then you might be willing to have your head transplanted to a healthy body, which is the thinking of this Russian gentleman. As the brain contains the mind, and the mind stores the memories, then obviously the mental life of the transplanted head continues. Hence if it were your head, you would go on living.

There are endless medical questions for which there are not yet any answers. How do you find the right matching body? How do you keep the head alive once decapitated? There are also psychological and ethical issues to face. To those in the profession it does not seem impossible, but to the uninitiated the whole idea seems quite impracticable.

There is a phrase from Rudyard Kipling's poem "*If*" that seems to apply here, "keep your head when others about you are losing theirs."

2.

Read a Book—Live Longer!

A friend indicated that she had read eight books in one month. I think that is commendable. She also walks, takes care of her husband and children, takes care of the house, provides lunches, cooks the meals, and all the other duties bestowed upon her as a wife and mother. She is also a regular contributor to Facebook. Yet I hear others say that they have no time to read. If I am not mistaken, I think it has something to do with desire.

I love to read. At one time I was reading an average of five or six books a month. May not sound like much but some were over 400 pages long. I assumed it helped my brain, and at my age it needs all the help I can give it. But reading for me is more than that. I find it expands my thinking, challenges my intellectual understanding, and enlarges my sphere of education.

We will never know everything, so to stop learning is to stunt further development of our minds. In fact, as you have probably discovered, the more we learn the less we seem to know. The mind is always open to receive more information and the brain is continually in the development mode. We can never overload our brains.

Harry Truman reportedly said, "Not all readers are leaders, but all leaders are readers." Interesting statement. Not sure that I would go with *all* leaders but a very high percentage of them have displayed the knowledge and understanding that could be attributed only to much reading.

I did a little research and discovered some interesting statistics. Reading holds many health benefits to both body and mind, however, the brain appears to be the greatest beneficiary. Scientific research shows that reading creates new neural pathways in the brain, causing new synapses to be created. This in turn increases the brain's elasticity, which reduces mental decline and improves memory capacity.

It has also been discovered that reading reduces stress far more effectively than even listening to music, taking a walk, or even quietly sitting with a cup of tea. The participants in the study were relaxed within six minutes when reading a book. It confirms this quotation by Richard Steele, "Reading is to the mind what exercise is to the body." Reading improves our thinking processes. It enhances our social skills and allows us to communicate better.

Reading for the elderly counters mental decline by as much as 32%. These same people were two-and-a-half times less likely to suffer from Alzheimer's. It is worth regular reading for that benefit alone. Even having someone read audibly to you has significant benefits.

Depressed patients have shown a positive improvement from such activity, and children particularly respond to it. The children show solid evidence of being able to think more logically and to grasp abstract concepts better.

It is hard to argue against the positive benefits of reading, yet I understand that North Americans read an average of two books a year. Sadly, if that is the average, then hundreds of thousands of people never read anything if others are reading 40 or 50 books a year. It was incredibly rewarding for a gentleman to say to me after having read my first book, "You did something that no one else has done. You caused me to read a book!" That coming from a man was significant. Men read far less than women. Mark Twain made a thought-provoking statement: "A person who won't read has no advantage over the one who can't read."

So what books should we read? Well, there are books which simply entertain and are humorous. They are good for us because laughter is a great medicine. They lift our spirit and make us feel good. However, books that cause us to think and question and provide a window on the world, its people, its science and discoveries, are invaluable. They help us to grow.

For writers, reading is essential. One well-known writer stated, "If you have no time to read, then you have no time to write." But I believe reading is essential for all of us, whether or not we want to write. Today we have no excuse. As you have probably heard, "Of the making of books there is no end." Whatever type of writing attracts you, there are books available at low prices, electronically and in print. And don't forget your local library.

So be entertained, be challenged, look into a new field and expand your mind. Put off the television, put on some music and get lost in a good book. Carry a book with you wherever you go. There are many wasted moments in the day.

Let the waiting rooms of the nation become the reading rooms of our souls. I am sure I read or heard that somewhere. It sounds good to me.

3.

Speak to Me... Please!

It is an understatement to say that we live in a technological age, for which we are mostly grateful. We now live with automation, drones, and robotics. Many factory assembly lines are totally automated. Robotics are used extensively in the medical field. Robots in the home and workplace are no longer fiction. Microchips surgically placed under the skin are already with us. One gentleman I saw had a chip embedded in his hand to unlock a door by the wave of his hand. Maybe he was afraid he would lose his keys. The argument is that we put chips in cats and dogs, so why not us? On a positive note, it's been suggested that these microchips could hold our medical history, so in an emergency situation that information would be readily available to medical personnel.

But I would like to say a few words about the humble cell phone which most of us own. Long gone are the days when to make an emergency call one had to find a public phone—and for those of us from England it used to be the red telephone box at the end of the street. Today our mobile phone gives immediate access to an emergency call. Communication between us today has never been so easy, so available, and so well used. But with all of that are we losing the art of communication?

Someone said to me that, sadly, young people are losing the ability to talk and discuss issues. Maybe some just don't want to. The ironic thing is they communicate with each other endlessly but in short words or abbreviated text messages. Using letters as an abbreviated sentence would indicate that time is of the essence. If so, why not a phone call? It would make more sense, because verbal communication is much faster, and what is more, the meaning is better understood because of the intonation within the voice. Maybe time is not the issue.

A teacher has said, "Young people are desperate for connections." I assume the obsession with the cell phone would confirm what he says. However, it does not seem to be a face-to-face connection. The cell phone is the instrument of choice. How many times have you seen four young people at a table in a restaurant, none of them talking to each other but all of them tapping away on their mobile devices? Obviously, the recipients of their messages were far more important than those with whom they were sitting. Maybe they were texting each other—who knows?

I saw a young couple come into a restaurant. They were shown to their table next to ours and they spoke not a word to each other. From the moment they sat down until their order was taken, they were engrossed in more important business on their smart phones. They stopped to place their order and immediately went back to texting. I am not certain whether they chatted at all over that meal, because their devices stayed right alongside their plates while eating.

Communication is essential to socializing, but it seems that the art of communicating is in decline. If we don't talk to people how will we ever really know how they are? I guess it begs the question, "Do we care?" How will we know when things are bothering them? How can we build relationships? If we choose to ignore a friend sitting next to us, I would venture to say that the friendship is in question or at best is very superficial. Perhaps we are moving away from friendships to acquaintances.

What about this as an act of discourtesy, if not rudeness. I saw a lady on her cell phone as she approached a cash desk in the store. She placed her clothing purchases on the counter, ready to pay. She held her phone between her shoulder and head, rummaged in her purse for a credit card, nodded to the cashier when asked a question, put her card through the machine, picked up the bag of clothes, and walked away still talking to a friend on the telephone. She said nothing to the lady who served her. Is that rude, discourteous, or disrespectful? Maybe all three.

I have seen a similar thing when people point to the menu when the waitress is attempting to serve them. One must wonder whether the communication on the telephone is so critical in nature as to disregard the human being who is offering his or her service. To act that way seems to say, "You are not important enough for me to talk to you."

Mobile devices are convenient. No problem having them available to connect with others, and especially in the event you are urgently needed, but should we allow them to stifle our communication with one another? Surely that defeats the purpose of owning them. Some families ban any technological device at the family meal table. A good idea.

Remember this, when it comes to our phones or any other devices, we own them, they don't own us! We must not allow them to rule our lives, ruin our friendships and take precedence over more important issues in life.

So let me urge you; look up occasionally, you might see someone who actually wants to talk!!

4.

Why Is Our World So Upside Down?

W hy is our world in such a mess? At the time of writing this you could choose any continent and you would find unrest—protests against governmental corruption and against authority, or you would find military conflict. It seems that few countries are exempt from potential trouble. The so-called Islamic State continues its relentless terrorist activities in Europe and other countries, killing hundreds at a time with suicide missions. Then hundreds, if not thousands more are killed—many beheaded—in areas of the Middle East.

The years of Syrian conflict brought nothing but devastation and suffering. What an ugly situation where cities have been destroyed and millions of people displaced, many of them forced to flee their country. Through no fault of their own, they have been driven out by tanks, bombs, the threat of death, and starvation. Some of them had to leave dead family members behind unburied. Most have escaped with nothing more than the clothes in which they were dressed. Now they are forced totally to rely upon the goodness of others to feed and care for them.

Hundreds of thousands of people from North Africa and other countries further east have risked crossing the Mediterranean using inadequate boats in an attempt to get to Europe as a safe haven from the ravages of war, persecution, and economic deprivation. Thousands did not make it but died making the crossing. Desperate people do desperate things.

We cannot help but be moved by the suffering of refugees. Having had experience working firsthand in areas of the world where refugees were prevalent, I came to realize something of the emotional upheaval and turmoil when a family is forced to leave their home, perhaps with only ten minutes' notice. What do you take? What do you leave? Most left everything because their lives, and those of their families, were more precious than any possessions.

And so it goes on. A diatribe of man's inhumanity to man. The death of one person is a tragedy. The death of hundreds is deplorable, and of thousands is inexcusable. I believe the problem lies deep within the collective human heart. It will not be until we recognize our insatiable greed, and hunger for power and domination, that things will actually begin to change.

Climate change also appears to be taking its toll. We read of constant storms and floods in some areas of the world, while drought brings hunger and concern in other places. Hence people are starving in Africa when there really is enough food to go around. The problem lies in its distribution. It is not unknown for food to be destroyed rather than sell it below market price for the less fortunate. How unjust can that be?

Why do we see such imbalance between crime and punishment in our court rooms? How is it we see one country give a young man a one-year sentence for murder, and even that sentence reduced by time waiting for the trial? Or how is it that in another country a man gets 21 years in prison for killing 79 people? That was the maximum under their law. On the other side of the issue, one young man is sentenced to 15 years' hard labor for stealing a poster. We seem to live in an age of injustice, where the suffering of the innocent is overlooked, or worse, ignored.

Did you know that God has something to say about this issue? Proverbs says that, "Acquitting the guilty and condemning the innocent—the Lord detests them both." Injustice is an abomination to God.

What can we do about the turmoil around us? What can we do about the injustice that is so prevalent? Regrettably, we can do very little in practical terms to eliminate drought and starvation. We can do nothing about the military conflicts around the world. Even the injustice is out of our reach to combat. We can hope and pray that our national and international leadership will have wisdom in applying practical solutions to the problems our society is encountering.

Can we as individuals make a difference? We can only look for opportunities that allow us to express our love and concern on a one-to-one basis. Thousands of families are being resettled in various countries. We can seek to help those who have been reduced to owning nothing more than the clothes on their backs. We can all give out of our abundance. We can find a mission or charitable organization which is helping to alleviate the suffering. Your small investment will produce large dividends.

Years ago, when I worked for a mission bringing aid to the poor, someone actually said to me, "Why do you bother, there is so much poverty, so much starvation, and there are so many refugees! Surely your efforts make very little impact." My answer was, "People suffer one at a time and we can help them one at a time."

5.

Refugee or Scoundrel?

I n February 1989 I met a young Polish refugee in his late twenties. He was intelligent and very pleasant. He had just arrived in Canada. Earlier in the day I had received a telephone call from a friend, asking if I would visit this young man, who was being detained by the immigration authorities in Toronto. Because of my mission experience in Poland, my friend thought it might be helpful for me to meet this new arrival. He was to await a refugee tribunal hearing.

The officer escorted me to a holding cell, where I was introduced to the young man. He was keen to tell me that he was a Christian and had escaped out of Poland because he was threatened with persecution. He said he had managed to get to Vienna, where a contact had given him an airline ticket to Canada. He said he had lost his passport.

I asked Immigration what it would take to get him released. They told me that by posting a $2,000 bond I could take him out while waiting for his hearing. I posted the bond and took him home—much to the surprise of my wife!

Word got out among the Christian community that he was in our home and people wanted to help. One lady spent over $300 on shoes and new clothes for him. Another bought him a winter coat. Many others made contributions. Our new-found friend became a very well dressed refugee.

Some other friends, who lived in another town, found him a job, but for this he needed to live with them. He received permission and so moved in with our friends. He made himself at home with them and began work.

About one month into this new phase, we received a call from our friends, indicating that the young man had been making regular telephone calls to the United States. There had been no indication from him that he knew anyone in Canada or the United States. We suggested that it might be wise to investigate further, maybe by calling those numbers. What we discovered was most disturbing.

He had not come from Poland. In fact, he had come from Germany, where he had abandoned his wife and child. He had destroyed his identity papers on the plane to Canada. The telephone calls to the United States were being made to a girlfriend.

Naturally we became concerned about his willingness to stay around for a refugee hearing. I was obligated to give the immigration authorities the information we had discovered, and even took him in to their office for his monthly check-in, as required. Although they had the information they did nothing. Two days later he disappeared.

We had all been deceived. He knew how to work the system. Because of his disappearance I soon received a notification from the Canadian Government threatening legal action if I did not pay up the $2,000 bond money. Government officials came to visit after his disappearance. Not sure whether they thought we were hiding him. The demand for payment was made more than once, even while in verbal and written discussions with them. Fortunately, I had documented everything, including the dates of my reports to them. After several attempts, I was able to get released from the bond liability.

Refugees are rarely out of the news and always in need of help, so our experience begs the question, "Would we do it again if presented with similar circumstances?" I think we would if we thought the person was in real need, but next time I think we might ask a few more questions!

6.

Whose Shoes Are You Wearing?

Are you a people watcher? Do you ever sit on a seat in the mall or in a park and just watch people go by? Do you look at their faces and wonder what is going on in their minds? Do you ever wonder what job they do or what kind of home life they have? Do our faces truly reflect what is going on in our lives?

These people who pass by come from various backgrounds. They all have differing circumstances, different occupations, and are probably wrestling with aspects of their own private situations. Each comes from a different family and has good and bad relationships within that family. They have friendships outside of their families, some congenial, some not.

It is an interesting pastime to try to determine what the facial expressions are saying, but it is nearly impossible to be correct. We cannot see beyond the face. We cannot see their pleasures or their problems. We have no idea of the stress or emotional pain they may be suffering at that moment. We cannot know the heartache they might be experiencing because of the illness or loss of a spouse or child. They may be going through the turmoil of a broken relationship or in the middle of a nasty divorce. This is why I say it is virtually impossible to read faces. They do not always portray the true inner feelings. Even those laughing could be covering their real hurt.

Let me tell you a true story. A gentleman had just taken his aisle seat on the plane when another man came along with two bags. He attempted to ram the bags in the overhead compartments, which were seemingly too small to accommodate his luggage. So he ranted and raved in impolite language while struggling with these bags. The gentleman already seated remonstrated with him suggesting he calm down and take it easy. The reply he received was not expected. The man said "Listen. Two of my daughters have just been in a serious car accident. One of them has died and the other is in serious condition. I am on my way to see them. How would you feel?"

This says to me that, until we walk in other people's shoes, we have no idea of the depth or intensity of their situation. Some are desperate at not finding a job, with bills piling up and a family to feed. Some may have just received an adverse medical report. I used to wonder why some people looked so unhappy, and then I realized that possibly they were unhappy! I have come to realize that I have no right to be judgmental on anyone's facial expression.

I've come to realize that if someone is a bit off, sullen, or even outright rude, there could be a good reason. I've learned to be more understanding and loving towards other people. I have no idea what is happening in their lives, no idea what might be troubling them, and no idea of the obstacles they might be facing.

As people age, one has little idea of what is going on in the mind. Changing circumstances and health issues have unexpected effects upon older people. In that situation, it is not out of the ordinary to receive an answer which is totally out of keeping with the person's personality. So let's not be quick to make a judgement call. Sometimes the unpleasant outburst or impatient comment may be hiding a deep hurt, repressed but not expressed. I have come to realize, that until I can read someone else's mind, I have no right to judge them by their facial expression.

Considering all this left me with a question; "What can I do to compensate?" or "What can I do to make a difference in their lives?" I concluded probably not a lot, and maybe nothing, but I realized I could do one thing. Rather than just sit there on a park bench and look as people pass by, I could offer a smile to those who look my way. May not seem much to us, but it could be to them. Sometimes the least we can do is the most we can do.

My wife and I were sitting in a restaurant one day, waiting for our food, when a gentleman came in and sat at another table. He finished his meal before us and on his way out came over and said to me, "I want to thank you. When I came in you gave me a very pleasant smile and it made me feel good. Thank you for that." It may not be much but it obviously makes a difference!

7.

Living in the Now

Eugene O'Kelly, the one-time CEO of KPMG, the large international accounting firm, authored a book entitled, *Chasing the Daylight*. He wrote it after he had been diagnosed with brain cancer and given three months to live. He had three tumors, each the size of a golf ball. Little could be done. To that point he had led a very active life and always enjoyed good health. The news came as an incredible shock. He died three-and-a-half months later. Fortunately, he suffered little pain, which helped him achieve what he wanted to do.

His strength of character and personality shone through as he prepared for his death. His actions were to "...make the time remaining the best of my life, and as good as it could possibly be for those most affected by my situation." I think he achieved that admirably.

The inevitable search for meaning in life was there and the recognition that, ultimately, the ownership of things is quite meaningless when faced with one's mortality. He looked at his business colleagues and wished they could understand that having the trappings and all the toys from climbing the corporate ladder was like chasing the wind. He wished they could see when enough was enough.

He took the time and made the effort to wind down, or bring to closure as many relationships as he could. He began with business colleagues and gradually moved on to close friends, immediate family, and then his wife and daughters. He wanted the closures to be positive and a time to share how important the relationships had been to him. Many he approached found it very difficult to say goodbye, and did not want to let go. Some could not accept the finality of it, while others became angry, thinking he was giving in too easily. His immediate family were given special times in meaningful places for their final goodbyes.

He talks about his transition from this life to the next and how he dealt with the sense of the unknown. However, in making the best of the situation he attempted to live in the now and not dwell on the past or even think of tomorrow. He found real purpose and meaning in living and enjoying each day, each hour. He basked in the pleasure of those special moments of being fully present, by taking in every little detail of his surroundings, much of which had previously passed unnoticed.

Eugene Kelly's book made an even greater impression when we heard about the passing of two men relatively young in age. I say *relatively* because both were nowhere near the age we associate with death. One was 41, the other 57. Both died of apparent heart attacks. Both were active and appeared healthy. Their deaths were a shock to all who knew them.

Some of us who are much older think of the privilege we have enjoyed in being with our families for the years we have been given. But my wife brought up an interesting question or statement. She said, "I wonder what the clock says as it relates to our lives?" Is it showing 11.30 pm or perhaps five minutes to midnight? We don't know and we will never know until the clock strikes twelve. Maybe it is better that we don't know.

Without morbidity, we have to face the issue that none of us knows what tomorrow holds for us. I am sure you have heard this before, but it is true, yesterday has gone, tomorrow never comes, we have only today. So use it we must. It is the only time we are given. Someone has said that life is a gift, that is why it is called the present. Maybe a play on words but it carries some truth.

All of this reminds us to live in the moment, express our genuine love to our family and to others for whom we care. We need to be sensitive to others and their situations. We need to do important things now while we have the time. We must live in the now because that is all we have! Looking at the final days of Eugene O'Kelly I thought, *what a superb example of making the most of his last moments.* It made me sit up and face the question, "How would I spend my last three months on earth?"

8.

The Bane of Negativity

I f ever there was a statement of negativity, it comes from Murphy. He was the man who birthed Murphy's law. Apparently he said, "Nothing is as easy as it looks; everything takes longer than you expect; and if anything can go wrong, it will and at the worst possible moment." There you have it, the philosophy which drives negativity. Although there may be an element of truth in it, the sweeping generalizations diminish the truth.

Negativity is insidious. It is a robber of joy and happiness. It causes one to be downbeat, skeptical, and always expecting the worst. It kills any spirit of optimism. Goals always appear beyond reach. Negativity feeds on negativity and it grows out of all proportion. The world contains so much negativity it is easy to become contaminated. We need to choose to walk away from it because the constant drip of negativity in our lives will eat away like dry-rot in a house.

However, few of us would openly acknowledge having a negative attitude. To counter such a suggestion the response is, "I'm not negative, I'm just being realistic!"

But being realistic is not the opposite of being positive! This is not to say that all negative statements are out of place. Some statements are realistic, sensible, and need to be said, even if they carry a negative message. But real negativity helps no one. It destroys goals, aspirations, and achievements. It creates a skewed view of oneself. It depletes self-esteem. It nullifies joyous living and reduces the quality of life. It limits possibility-thinking, keeping us trapped in our comfort zone.

Now you might be saying, "It's all right for you, you don't know what I have to put up with from life." Well, that may not be quite true. I find looking after my wife twenty-four hours a day, seven days a week, is no small task. It is hard to see the health of your spouse deteriorate. It would be easy to become negative about the situation. However, to be negative would not help. In fact, it would make matters worse, especially mentally. It would be nothing more than a pity party. How much better to look for the good, for the positive, and live in hope that things will improve?

I believe that negativity takes away the spark of life. It sees only the downside of life. It looks at the faults and not the achievements. It sees the worst side of every situation and expects a negative outcome. Perhaps negative people think that, if things turn out better than expected, that would be a bonus.

Negativity can have a detrimental effect on health as it produces an increase in stress, which can then bring about adverse medical conditions, among them some stomach or digestive problems. Once a negative attitude gets a grip, it is difficult, but not impossible, to remove. We cannot control what experiences come into our lives, be they positive or negative, but we can control our reaction or response to them.

You know the excuses: "I can't do it," "I think it is too much for me," "I am afraid I will make a mess of things," "I am afraid of what people might think of me," and so on. Consequently, ideas get deferred or written off completely. "I can't" is one of the most powerful negative phrases. I tend to believe that because it closes the door to potentiality.

Someone once said, "If you think you can, you are right. If you think you can't, you are also right." If the predominant aspect of our thinking says, "I can't," then the possibility of any worthwhile achievement diminishes quickly.

What's behind all this negativity? Why do we allow our minds to run along these tracks? It is fear, plain and simple. Fear creates negativity—fear of risk, fear of the unknown, fear of failure, fear of people, fear that all will not work out exactly as we hope or plan.

Situations and circumstances are often unchangeable. We cannot change people. Many aspects of life are beyond our control, so it does no good for us to dwell on that which we cannot change. We need to face it, rise above it, overcome it, and not let it defeat us. We need to seek the positive in every situation. No one tells us how to think or what to think. We are in control of our thinking and our attitude. We can blame no one else. We can choose not to be negative.

So let's look for the good, see the best, think the best, think optimistically, and go with the flow. Brighten up your day. Think positively and allow things to fall into place—they usually do.

9.

The Power of Positivity

I f anyone had reason for a pity party or to suffer from the "poor me" syndrome, it was Bethany Hamilton. The thirteen-year-old lost an arm to a shark while surfing in Hawaii. She refused to be negative about the accident. Only ten weeks later she was surfing again at national competition level and came fifth in her age category. How positive is that?

Positive thinking brings opportunities; it creates optimism; it allows us to overcome serious obstacles. We can think big and entertain possibility-thinking. It creates an attitude of, "I can do this if I put my mind to it." Positivity creates and maintains motivation so that we can achieve more., "where your attention goes, your energy flows." Where we place our attention and energy we normally get results. Goals become more believable and achievable. One sees the good and recognizes the potential. Positiveness brings with it a brighter outlook.

A negative attitude produces the exact opposite. It finds obstructions. It sees hurdles where there are no hurdles. A negative view of oneself is like a mountain. But mountains are not insurmountable. In fact, with a positive attitude, mountains can become molehills. The road ahead may still be uphill, but you sense the wind in your back.

It would be nonsense to suggest that having a positive attitude removes all problems and obstacles because that is not true. We still have to face circumstances that cause concern, but somehow the worry and stress aspect seems to be reduced. Positivity allows us to face adverse situations and obstacles with logic and sensibility, and provides strength and support to rise above them. Possibilities are recognized which may normally have been overlooked.

I once read about a man who lived just outside Chicago and was laid off from work. It was winter and difficult to find other work. Instead of sitting at home bemoaning his fate, he went out for walks and tried to think through his situation. On one of those walks he discovered an elderly lady trapped in her house because there was no one to clear the snow. He freely shoveled her driveway. Noticing that, a neighbor asked him to shovel her driveway, then another, and another. They willingly paid him, which helped pay his bills.

Spring came and he was asked to do clean-up work, including clearing basements of unwanted items, some of which he discovered were antiques. The end result was he became the owner of a landscaping business and an antique store, earning far more than his previous job. He said getting laid off was the best thing that ever happened to him.

Positive expectations go a long way to arriving at

your goal and achieving your long-term objective. Do we go into each day expecting it to be a positive day? Do we expect that the things we do and the people we meet will make a positive contribution to our day? Are we looking for it? Do we expect it? Our attitude makes the difference. We can't help what life throws at us. I guess the secret is how we face it and handle it. Positivity goes hand in hand with optimism. Positivity creates attitude, a winning attitude, one which is admired and appreciated.

The man in Chicago could have sat at home feeling sorry for himself, waiting for someone else to pull him out of the slump he was in. His attitude did not allow that. He acted positively and gained a good result and massive benefits he would never had known had he not taken a positive initiative.

Numerous studies have shown that when the participants received positive input about themselves they achieved higher and better results in examinations. Their expectations of themselves produced better responses, made them feel better, happier, and more fulfilled. Positive comments can make an amazing difference.

Positivity brings with it a healthier life and a more vibrant and outgoing attitude. It creates a disposition with which it is difficult to be down or depressed. It helps to build belief in oneself that can change "not me" into "why not me?" It makes it possible to see and achieve success.

Even if we never experienced it, we all know of someone who was "put down" as a child. It was made very clear to them that they would achieve very little in life. Unfortunately, with the suggestibility of a young mind it was a self-fulfilling prophecy, with many struggling to be accepted and to find confidence in their abilities. However, not all succumbed to that prediction. Some saw the folly of the false assumptions and set out to achieve a life of usefulness and accomplishment. The benefits of praise in a child's life are enormous. Positivity in childhood in the form of encouragement and support produces a legacy of good self-esteem, self-assurance, and confidence to face issues of living.

A positive attitude is the key. If we think positively, use positive words, and refuse to accept negativity, we will win every time.

10.

Maybe the Tortoise Was On to Something

I found the book, "*In Praise of Slow,*" by Carl Honoré, most fascinating and thought-provoking. It portrayed our present society as being in a hurry and wanting everything in an instant—from instant coffee, to instant printing, faster internet, and many other things for which we have no time to wait. It showed a society with a lack of patience and displaying the inability to "slow down and smell the roses."

The author outlined many different facets of our lives where we could or should consider slowing down. He covered aspects that readily come to mind, such as driving, but he also mentioned other aspects we don't so readily think of as being rushed. I am sure we appreciate that slowing down in most areas holds incredible benefits for all of us, including emotional and mental health issues.

Slow down on the roads. Which of us keeps within the speed limits? Yet we know that by doing so, fewer people would be injured and more people would be alive. To slow down in our eating habits, by eating more together as families, and by taking the time to enjoy the food, will not only do our digestive system good but will have long-term effects upon our health. It also brings closer relationships within the family. Sadly, many families only eat together when they go to McDonalds, with the average time at the table being eleven minutes. Hence the appropriate title of "fast-food." We are reminded that the French and Italians willingly sit on the patios of roadside cafés for hours and let the world go by, as they enjoy their coffee.

The book also touches on the area of medicine, where the author examines the doctor-patient relationship, along with the disbursement of medical advice. It suggests that the demand for speed forces doctors to give less attention to the patient than what they would like to, and probably what they need to.

Education is another area, in which the statistics show the benefits of slowness in achievement. Individual attention to the student, such as in home schooling, gives a child the opportunity to study at his or her own speed and often offers an advantage over other regular schooling situations.

The author scrutinizes other aspects of our lives that could benefit from slowing down. He covers the bedroom, the work place, and our times of leisure, pointing out the advantages of pulling away from the frenetic lifestyle we live to a more measured pace in all things.

Do you remember when the computer first appeared in the workplace and it was said it would give us more free time? It was even suggested that we would be working a four-day week. That never happened. Our lives are just as busy, if not busier, as we crowd more and more activities into the hours available. It takes discipline to switch off and focus attention on the important as opposed to the urgent. It is a good idea to say "no" occasionally. We need to dissect our schedules. Create downtime—maybe for doing nothing. Perhaps put our feet up and stare into space. Slowing down brings a whole better perspective on life. Meditation is also another recommended activity now and is even encouraged and practiced at corporate level.

The thesis of slowing down is a good one and well worth considering. There are those, however, who perhaps should speed up, but for most of us slowing down to enjoy life cannot be a bad thing. Taking time to be with family. We may be moving too fast and missing life's special and precious moments. They are often not repeated. Putting busyness on hold to spend time with our spouse, our children or grandchildren may take effort, and even organizing, but they will love us for it because it shows we care. It might mean making eating together an event, as opposed to simply a necessity. This must pay off in the long run.

I am sure we all know that simply to sit in silence and enjoy a sunset, or take in the sight of beautiful flowers, the cherry blossoms, or other aspects of creation, gives us a real sense of serenity, peace, and satisfaction.

So today why not make the decision to slow down? Just sit and think, read, write, talk, discuss, and dream. Enjoy the company of others. Give them your full attention, especially your children. Life will go on just the same whether we slow down or not, but by slowing down, it will become more meaningful and your mental health will thank you for it!

II.

Think Twice, Choose Once

Ｎone of us is exempt from making choices. If we are human we have no option. From the time we wake up to the time we go to sleep, our lives are governed by choices, and this continues throughout life. We make choices, some small, some big, some good, some bad, but the end result is the same—we have to live with the results of those choices, be they bitter or sweet. Fortunately, some choices can be changed, the situation can be reversed, but regretfully that is not the same for all our decisions.

Many things we choose are common place and insignificant, but major life choices can be, and usually are, extremely important and can have a far-reaching affect, both on us and other people. When we were young we had no concept of what our decisions then might bring about later in life. However, I am sure we made them with the best intention and understanding we had at the time. We are where we are today because of decisions made yesterday or maybe long ago.

Our choice of relationships, our choice of education, our career, of where we live, where we go to church;

they all play essential parts in our life. They all influence our enjoyment of life or the opposite. They influence our level of content or discontent. They create satisfaction or dissatisfaction. Such are the long tentacles of choice-making.

Choices can make us or break us. Take just one simple example. If we eat too much cake or too many desserts and do no exercise then that choice will bring its own result! However, if we do the opposite – fewer desserts and more exercise, as painful as that is, that will bring its own reward. One piece of cake or one dessert seems innocent enough, but have you ever tried to picture 365 pieces of cake—one for each day of the year—what a pile of cake that would be? What about 365 desserts? What a wonderful array of delights to feast upon but horrendous when you think that over the last twelve months they have been consumed.

Choices are not always easy to make. Realizing the ramifications for the future based upon your decision of today—the future being unknown and untested—the choice becomes critically important. Tomorrow will be the result of today's choices. Even very small decisions can have lifelong and devastating consequences.

I read about a lady in South America who had a premonition about a journey she was to go on. She told her family they should not go, but the family overruled. The car was in an accident. The lady was seriously injured. Her unborn baby had to be delivered prematurely and weighed just four pounds. Mother and child survived but a choice by the family brought untold suffering. How many people have made the decision of just one more drink with disastrous results? How many people have made a choice to go somewhere only to find themselves in the wrong place at the wrong time?

Think about the choice of marriage. Who you marry is an important decision. If you have children they then are peculiar to your marriage, to you and your spouse. Have you ever thought that if you had not married your particular spouse then those children would never have existed? Not a nice thought when you think how special your children are to you. Another aspect is this. If you had married someone else, your whole life may have gone down a completely different path, especially if some choices had been made together. The marriage vows indicate a commitment for life. That's how serious finding the right marriage partner is. Life is a long time. It certainly is a scenario where the saying, "Choose in haste, regret at leisure," applies.

Some people say that divorce has helped to correct many wrong decisions. Sadly, it is true that time has revealed for some the person they married turned out to be completely different from pre-marriage days. Some couples have made the choice to stay in their marriage for the sake of their children, although time has proven that divorce may have been the better and right course. Many have opted for a trial marriage or just living together, but the rate of breakup, or divorce if they married, is identical in proportion to regular married people. All this to say that decisions for marriage partners or decisions for divorce all have long-term and far reaching reverberations touching many lives, as the effects expand in concentric circles.

Obviously, we have no idea of the ultimate outcome or end result of our decisions, and all contingencies cannot be covered. We need wisdom at all times. The choices we make in life are our own responsibility. There is no blame game here. All decisions are best made thoughtfully, intelligently, and without sudden impulse. However, we have no option; we have to make choices. To do nothing is also a choice.

So whatever choices we make on this journey of life, remember: we will always enjoy or endure the result. To ensure a good result, we consider all the implications involve—upon us, our family, and upon others in our circle of friends. Decisions are often larger than we imagine. Think twice, choose once—excellent advice.

12.

Where Is Your Mind Now?

Here's a hard question to answer. Do we live mindfully or mindlessly? Most of us likely vacillate between the two. Do we do most things out of habit or do we think things through before we act? Ellen J. Langer, professor of psychology at Harvard University, has written a book titled *Mindfulness*. One reviewer calls the content, "A life-enhancing alternative... the antidote to the rigid, reactive, repetitive patterns that keep the best of us sealed in unlived lives." What an incredible and heavy statement! Do we really live unlived lives?

The essence of the book is that a good chunk of us live mindless lives. We may immediately object to such a supposition, but are we really totally observant to that which is around us? Do we miss the details because we concentrate on the big picture? Do we actually see what we look at? The answer to these questions will determine our mindfulness or lack of it. The premise of the suggestion that we are unmindful is the untold evidence from research that many people respond and act without due consideration to the real issue before them. In other words, we do things so often without thinking.

The book gives an example of two pilots going over their pre-flight checklist. Because they were used to flying in warm climates they checked that the deicer was switched off, as normal, but their flight on this occasion took them into cold weather. The plane iced up and crashed. They were doing what they normally do regularly and were not mindful of the flight before them.

Think about it; how much of our present actions are related to our past? I would hazard a guess and say pretty much all of them. We have no option but react and respond according to the events and experience in our past. Our thinking is shaped by our experience. A grid system has been created through which everything passes. It has been formulated by our past associations and experience. Thus, everything that comes to us is automatically filtered through that system.

The book is an eye-opener as it covers mindlessness and mindfulness in many scenarios of life. It looks at the roots and nature of mindlessness as well as mindfulness in work-related situations and health issues. It portrays the diversity of its application and infers we miss out if we live in that state of mindlessness.

We discover from the book that because we mostly act and speak out of our previously established set of habits, we find ourselves blindly following routine thinking and patterns. This is seen in our reactions or responses to questions and situations presented to us. Instead, we should be evaluating the question in real time and intelligently thinking through the best answer or solution to the current situation.

Do we really listen to questions or statements being made to us, or are we too busy preparing an answer for what we assume the question to be? The same question relates to what we see on television or hear on the radio. Do we simply accept everything without thinking it through? Do we ever question a question? Do we ever question a statement? If we do, then we are probably being a little more mindful and living in the present.

We obviously need to train ourselves to live in the now. We need to be present at every conversation. We need to be constantly mindful, which means reacting with the conscious brain and not necessarily coming out with a quick conclusion based upon experience. We need to think through the logic or ultimate consequence of our response or statement.

Generally, we are what some have called, "victims of time," which means we dwell on what was, what might have been, or what could have been, or looking into the future, what might be, what could be or what will be. However, the past no longer exists, the future also does not exist, the present is all that is real and it is all we have. If we give ourselves to intentional living it will reduce stress and bring the consequent health benefits with it. Mindful people tend to be happier, self-confident, and secure, accompanied by a greater ability to face and overcome obstacles.

What is our answer to, "Do I live in the now?" If we are honest we would say that most of us live in the past or in the future. We allow our minds to concentrate on the events of yesterday or tomorrow's agenda. To live truly in the now means we would concentrate our attention as to what is in front of us and what surrounds us. We would actually observe what is taking place before us. We would not allow the activities of the past and the potential cares of the future to be a cause for us to miss the joy of the present. So let's live in the present and enjoy it. We can be in only one of two mindsets, mindful or mindless. Which mindset are you in right now?

13.

Time and Space

D oes time exist in space? We could argue that time does not exist anywhere but we have all come to recognize and accept that our lives are measured in linear time. That being so, time is probably the most precious commodity we have. It is limited. It is linear. It has a beginning and an end for each of us. It is like the spoken word and the sped arrow, once gone, they cannot be retrieved, they never return. Yet do we treat time with such value?

We can't stop time. It is the irreversible progress of our existence and a constant succession of events from the past into the future. Time moves only one way. Yet do we really consider its scarcity? I am sure there are times we think it expendable, times when we thoughtlessly use it up with undue consideration.

For hundreds of years a host of philosophers have studied the subject of time. Even the renowned Augustine studied time in the hope of understanding it and its affects upon human kind. We are all restricted by time and space. It doesn't matter who we are, whether the Queen, the Prime Minister or a mechanic in the workshop, we all have the same amount of time, 1440 minutes in each day and 168 hours per week. How we use those minutes is as varied as we are.

Our restriction in space is that we can be in only one place at any given moment. Therefore, we have this fence around our lives. Some people try to extend the fence. They expand the day by getting up very early and working long into the night. Some plan such tight schedules they almost expect their body to be in two places simultaneously. That is simply expanding the work hours in the day, not time itself. Time ultimately wins. We all are equal when it comes to the time we have but not equal in the use of that time, and that is what counts. Many people regret their use of time when they come to the end of their life, wishing they had given more time to family and other important issues within their lives. Time is precious. Once used it cannot be replaced.

Looking back over our lives we might now think it a tragedy how much time we may have wasted. We are a society of watchers. The average North American spends hours each day watching television, much of which would offer very little by way of positive contribution to their lives. However, relaxation is necessary and varies according to different people. It might be reading, it might be golfing or playing tennis, it could be watching television (sometimes falling asleep while doing so), or it may be just valued conversation or family time. That is not wasted time as rest is essential. Otherwise we simply burn out.

Our family relationships and other friendships are

restricted in their development by time and space. We have only so much time to spend with people so we need to allocate it wisely and build good relationships. The space aspect also becomes a hindrance when one is 3,000 miles from family or friends. The geography makes it difficult to spend face-to-face time with others. However, modern technology has helped.

We sometimes read criticism of Facebook, how it is a waste of time and a vehicle for people's mindless comments. Technology in itself is not the instigator of time wasted but how each of us uses that technology. If used correctly Facebook can make a positive contribution to our lives. It offers the opportunity to connect with family and friends far more often than if our contact were solely through email and the telephone—hence the name *social media*. In one three-month period I spoke to, and heard from, numerous people who probably didn't even know I was still on this earth. Facebook has facilitated renewed friendships and closer family connections.

Back to our subject, time and space. Hugh Ross, in his book *Why the Universe is the Way it Is* talks about our limitations caused by time and space. It showed me that we have to be good stewards of whatever we have, including time. It caused me to question how I use time. Do I use it wisely? Am I being selfish with it? Am I using it solely for my benefit or for the benefit of others like family and friends?

All these are questions worthwhile considering. How do we use our time? How are we using up our lives? We only have one life, and who knows how long that will be?

Let's make the most of it now, while we have the time. Time is of the essence.

I do like the following statement: "Live each day as though it is your last. One day you will be right."

14.

Real Friends Are Like Diamonds—Priceless

In 1964 my wife struck up a friendship with a young lady with whom she worked at that time. Today they are still regularly in contact. They have faithfully kept in touch over those years, although, for the most part, they have been separated by 3,000 miles, and for ten years, 6,000 miles. Today we live one-hour's drive away, so visits are the order of the day. Their bonding through the years got me thinking about friendships.

Friendships are invaluable. We've all heard the adage that you don't miss something until it is no longer there. That is so true with friendships. Having lived in Ontario, in central Canada, for over thirty years, we moved to British Columbia, on the West coast, several years ago and we quickly realized that, although we love being close to family and would not change that, it highlighted the importance of the friendships we had built in other places. Not only did we miss them as friends and people, it was as though we left something of ourselves behind. Although connections are maintained there is nothing to compare with face-to-face contact.

When we think of all the people that have come across our paths down the years, we realize how impossible it would have been to stay in touch with everyone. We often wonder where some of those wonderful people are now. Even the Christmas card list seems to get smaller each year.

Facebook has helped to reignite some of those friendships. I have spoken to and renewed friendships with many people from our past, something which never would have happened had I not overcome my resistance and made the effort to start using that form of social media.

Well, what is a true friend? We are not talking here about casual friendships of people who come into our lives and quickly disappear. Nor are we talking about work colleagues and others with whom we regularly pass the time of day. Acquaintances are numerous but true friends are few.

Friends are those with whom we have invested time and effort to be with regularly and enjoy their company. This builds understanding and trust. It has been said that a real friend is someone who knows all about you and loves you anyway. Real friendship does not change with fluctuating circumstances. A real friend will stand by you, will stand with you and will uphold you in the tough times. It is seen in their kindness, their empathy, and their love. They will bail you out in the times of hardship and will be there to lift you up when you fall down. Such friends will give support at the best of times and at the worst of times. They will give and not look for compensation.

Honesty is a mark of a true friend, honesty about us and them. The friendship is not threatened by an honest exchange. They are good listeners and responders to our conversation. Because of their sense of understanding just being in their presence can alleviate stress, such is the value of a deep friendship.

In times of crises true friends rise to the top like cream on milk. They are there at a moment's notice. They don't have to think about it. They rush to be by your side. It's at those times that we find ourselves astounded at the sacrifice they are willing to make to help us, simply because of our long and deep relationship.

I remember the faithfulness of a pastor friend who spent so much time with me out of his busy life when I was informed I had a tumor. As my wife did not drive at that time, it was he who took me to the hospital and it was he who was there to take me home. That was in 1988 but the memory of such kindness stays with one forever. My expressed gratefulness seemed so inadequate.

I hope you have such friendships in your life. If so, hang on to them. They are like diamonds - priceless. Think what those friendships have meant to you over the years, just by them being there for you at the right time. The value of true friends can never be overestimated.

The cost of losing friends is greater than the effort needed to keep them. We are social beings, as reflected in the success of social media; we enjoy real, true friendship. We need to value those friendships and keep them. It's harder to begin new relationships than keep the flame alive of the more established ones. Good friends are hard to replace.

15.

In Praise of Marriage

I used to think that golden wedding anniversaries were for old people; now I would like to think differently. In fact, we are only half a decade from the next big celebratory milestone—the diamond.

Believe me, the years float by like white clouds on a summer's day. However, it is impossible to go through life simply enjoying summer days. The storms of disappointments and financial struggles come and gratefully go. We can attest to having been given grace and fortitude to face sickness. Happily, there has been more laughter than tears, although both are appropriate in their place. It is said that adversity binds you together or rips you apart. Fortunately, it has been the former for us.

The question asked of people who have longevity in life or marriage is the proverbial, "What's the secret?" I don't think there is a secret. In marriage, love, commitment and communication have to be the order of the day. Commitments are made to be honored. A word or promise is to be kept. Trust is the result and the reward. I have also learned a few other aspects along the way.

Understanding: Misunderstanding is the primary cause of conflict and division. Try to understand your spouse. This may sound trite but it takes an investment of time and effort as well as patience. Find out what makes them tick. Why they think the way they do. Why they act the way they do. Discover what motivates them and what pleases them. Take note of that which annoys them (this one you tend to learn fast). Knowing the dominant aspects of your spouse's personality will put you far ahead in your understanding and acceptance of who they are.

Learn what is important: Despite having a good understanding, no two people can live together without running into conflict—unless one is totally subservient. At the time of disagreement one needs quickly to assess what is important and what is not. Am I being selfish? Am I pushing something which in a very short time will be insignificant? How many of our arguments and differences will have no consequence in a year or maybe a month or two? Important are those things which may have a long-term effect upon the marriage and the relationship.

Independence: Although in many ways the two become one—for instance in likes and dislikes and the enjoyment of entertainment—both are still individuals with different interests. That independence must remain to the degree that each spouse is allowed to be himself or herself and pursue those other interests, unless one of them becomes disruptive and holds the marriage relationship in complete disregard. The ongoing closeness in any relationship does not negate differences of views and concepts. Each must have that liberty to continue in his or her own individualistic thinking.

Consideration: Acts of kindness and thoughtfulness are not just appreciated, but highly valued. Sometimes they are worth more than a diamond ring—maybe that's pushing it, but they certainly are high on the approval list. Patience is another virtue which brings its own rewards. Because throughout our lives, and particularly in pre-marriage days, life revolved around us as individuals, it is hard to move away from that thinking and replace it with your spouse. Once married, life is not about you but it is predominantly about your spouse. When this attitude is cultivated and reciprocated life works well.

Friendship: This is one of the secrets to a long and happy marriage. Real friendship between spouses is crucial for all the hours spent together. To see the blemishes and overlook them or to see the faults and lovingly suggest correction. To share together, to laugh together, to discuss together, not always agreeing but without recrimination, makes a relationship strong and secure. If you have a spouse who is your best friend, then you are doubly blessed.

Consistency: Finally, no successful marriage can exist without consistent work on the relationship. Love builds over the years, but having made the commitment it still takes work to ensure its success. None of us is perfect and we will always make mistakes. Forgiveness and understanding are always precursors to harmony. If the marriage was meaningful in the first place, then it is worthwhile to keep that significant relationship moving along in a pleasant state of enjoyment.

This just scratches the surface but we'll leave it there because I, too, am still learning.

16.

The Elderly Are People Too

A re you old enough to remember the days when, as young people, we would think in terms of an old man or an old lady of 60? Well, now that I am eighteen years past that age, I naturally think differently. I have come to prefer the word *mature* rather than *old* or *elderly*. It is said that seniors always consider elderly to be ten years beyond their present age—a good concept.

Transition into old age is not easy. No change is easy. Even young people are happier in their comfort zone. However, the passing of time leaves us no choice but to accept life as it is and in consequence accept change as inevitable. How it is handled depends upon our attitude. We have to look for the best, embrace the good, and deal with the not-so-good. The not-so-good, however, can be caused by the attitude of the general populace. The elderly are often looked at in a negative light.

Some people consider being old as those close to or even surpassing the generally accepted life expectancy. Yet it is neither a biological or chronological function of the years one has lived, or even the physiological changes related to those years, but it tends more to be a social concept. Generally, if you ask seniors, you find that they do not feel their actual age. It is usually the feeling of a 40-year-old mind in a 70-year-old body although many older people will express satisfaction and fulfillment in their life regardless of how old they feel.

Whatever you think about the words *old* or *elderly*, I have learned that seniors cannot be categorized into one big group and labeled as being past their shelf-life date. Probably the biggest disservice rendered to seniors is the equating of physical incapacity with mental abilities. The two should never be equated. The agility of the mind is unrelated to the mobility of the body.

I can attest to this disservice when my wife, who has severe mobility problems, attempts to order her food in a restaurant. I get the third person "she' or "her' response such as, "What would she want?" or "What about her?" as though she cannot speak for herself. I give a very simple but gentle answer. "'Her' has a name and it is Rita and she is quite competent to make her own decisions." Rita has all her mental faculties, is sharp as a tack and has not lost her wit or sense of humor. Unfortunately, because of her lack of mobility, there are those who insist that her physical condition conveys mental incapacity, which is far from the truth. Regrettably, this is a common occurrence.

We are not alone in this. A friend who has now passed on experienced the same thing. He used a walker or a cane, but when eating out with his daughter she was always asked what her father would like. It was not until he got out his credit card to pay the bill that it was recognized that he had some semblance of intelligence.

It cannot be emphasized too much; mental deficiencies should never be equated with physical disabilities.

Sadly, the concept many have of the elderly is that they have run their course, are now worn out, and should be treated accordingly. All they need is rest and care. They need to be allowed to sleep at will, sit around or putter in the garden, passing the time. Nothing could be further from the truth. Care, yes, but activity is the name of the game.

The elderly are people too and they love to walk and to read. They devour the newspapers and magazines. They love to discuss and debate. They love to be active and get the most out of life. It is true that some of us lack in physical capabilities, but what is lost there is often made up in mental abilities. The elderly are not a bunch of physically decrepit psychological misfits. They are people who love life, who socialize, who enjoy a joke, and know what they like and dislike. Plus, they have a wealth of knowledge and experience to offer.

Some forgetfulness may be in the mix, but I know people in their forties who cannot remember names and faces or telephone numbers. Yet I know seniors who can. It is not solely an age thing. So, folks, don't write us old folks off as though we are finished. We may have reached our "best before" date but our "shelf life" has not expired. We are not yet done with life.

It is true that we may not be able to run the 100-yard dash as fast as we once could, but bring on a scrabble challenge and that may be a different story!

17.

How Many Heart Beats Do You Have Left?

Rob Dunn has written an interesting book entitled, *The man who touched his own heart!* It is a fascinating account of the history and development of the heart, its diseases and treatments. The title comes from the surgeon who first probed the heart through an artery. He did it to himself to prove that it could be done. His assistant volunteered for the experiment, but while the assistant was unconscious the surgeon performed the exercise on himself, not wanting anyone else to be exposed to the unknown risks involved.

As humans, our hearts average 70 to 80 beats per minute. Incredibly, hummingbirds exceed 1,200 beats per minute while flying, but fewer than 30 when resting. Whales can have as few as three beats per minute, hence their propensity to long life, often beyond 100 years.

Most animals have about one billion heartbeats over their lifetime. Humans used to have the same, but since our life span has increased those potential beats have now increased to around two billion. Right now you are probably doing some mental calculations to see how many heart beats you may have left. The good thing is that none of us knows.

For centuries, the medical profession held a highly-respected view of the heart. In fact, that respect was so high that the heart was off limits when it came to operating. About 60 years ago the medical profession became keenly interested in the possibility of heart transplants. Apparently, competition was fierce among surgeons to be the first in the execution of open heart surgery, and even more so to be the first in transplanting a heart. In their race to achieve success, surgeons did numerous trial runs on animals. They even transplanted the heart of a chimpanzee into a man and a man's heart into a chimpanzee. Both died within a few hours.

Then on December 3rd, 1967, in South Africa, the first open heart surgery took place. A donor heart became available through an accident, while a needy recipient had been waiting for months. Christiaan Barnard, assisted by his brother Marius, performed the first human to human heart transplant. The patient lived for 18 days.

Two other heart transplant pioneers, Richard Lower and Norman Shumway from the USA, had planned to wait several more years until they felt certain about having adequate knowledge and medical proficiency for the operation. However, pushed by Barnard's action they began performing heart transplants and became the recognized leaders in the field. By 1970, three years later, 175 heart transplants had taken place but only 23 people remained alive. It was even suggested that some of those people might have survived longer had they not had the operation. Today there are literally thousands of heart operations around the world with the implanting of the stent being the most common.

Behind the scenes of heart transplants were those whose desire and objective was to create an artificial heart. Incredible problems had to be overcome. They were trying to replace a live organ operating with its own electrical impulse. Various devices were invented, powered by external electrical current, but to no avail. Then during the 1970s Dr. William Kolff, William DeVries and Robert Jarvik began work on an artificial heart. It was called the Jarvik-7 heart. Kolff and Devries installed the first one into Barney Clark in 1987. Clark lived for 112 days. Many of those days he was not conscious and when he was he wanted to die. The second one installed allowed the patient to live 620 days. Most of the installations later kept people alive for months and some a few years. Some devices needed backpacks of batteries to operate, with the batteries constantly needing to be recharged. Although research and experimentation continue, the artificial heart has not replaced live heart transplants.

To this point, Rob Dunn's book was producing some very fascinating stuff, but then it got into the evolution of the heart as it related to Evolution. Maybe for some people this would prove to be of real interest but I found it not so. It is probably my bias but I find it difficult to understand how well-educated and respected scientists simply accept that we all came from the proverbial primordial soup. It all started with one cell somewhere and then over time—billions of years later—here we are fully developed but still evolving.

I have always left the evolution debate to the more scientifically-minded people to thrash out, but as I read this book it seemed that it took a greater faith to believe what I was reading than the story of creation, whatever your version of creation is. If the theory of evolution is true who launched the process?

According to the book, it was the lungfish which first ventured out of the water, walked on its fins for a bit until it grew legs. It then developed into something else and so commenced the process of animal life and ultimately us human beings. It's all a little mystifying why the lungfish would suddenly decide to take a walk up the beach and also why all his mates stayed behind in the water. I guess Mrs. Lungfish had to go with him, otherwise there would have been no little lungfishes to evolve.

That supposedly took place 360 million years ago. Then very recently, like eight million years ago, we humans branched out from the gorillas. How they know this is also a bit of a mystery. However, even given millions of years in the development it is difficult to see how a lungfish could grow into an elephant.

I think I may be out of my depth here, but I do find it confusing that elephants go on having elephants, gorillas have gorillas, and humans have humans. I thought that if we came from gorillas there would be no more gorillas. Maybe someone can enlighten me.

We are told that we are still evolving. Not sure about

you but I must be running out of time because all I have
seen is that I have evolved into old age.

18.

Do You Know Who I Am?

Have you ever been asked the question, "Who are you?" I wonder what your answer was. When I have asked people that question the immediate natural answer they give me is their name. I then indicate that their name is not who they are. The name is just a label to distinguish them from others but that is not their true identity. It has nothing to do with their personality, their character, or how other people perceive them. It does not determine or describe their psychological make-up, their persona or even their attitude to life.

Who we are has been shaped by our past. Our upbringing, our family background, our schooling and many other events and experiences along life's road have caused us to become who we are today. We could say that we are the sum total of our life experience. Our relationships are built on who we are. People accept us for who they think we are.

Several years ago, I ran into a television presenter. On his program and elsewhere he was always known simply by his first name. So I said, "Hello Brian," (not his real name). He looked at me as though I were an alien from space and replied, "Do I know you?" I answered "No, but I know you!" With not so much as a, "Nice to meet you," he moved on, ignoring my greeting. Obviously, it proved I was wrong. I knew of him but I didn't really know him.

The question he asked of me, "Do I know you?" is an interesting one. It made me wonder how well people know each other.

A while ago I had coffee almost every week with a friend. We would discuss many issues of life and especially things that applied to our own personal and family life. I learned from him his thinking on many subjects but did I really know him? Likewise, he heard my views and opinions on many topics, but could he say he really knew me? It is not uncommon for a small group of men, or even one-on-one, to meet and over breakfast have an accountability session. It creates an environment where events, thoughts, and feelings can be shared. An opportunity to unload a concern or seek advice on a difficult issue. A place to gain and feel supported.

It is probably true to say that we all know of many people but few of us really know each other well. It is rare that we share our deepest thoughts. For the most part we talk how we think others would expect us to talk. The private person remains private. Open and honest conversation, coupled with the knowledge that criticism is not even a remote possibility, are the foundational blocks on which to build a friendship of love, trust, and support. If there is criticism, it is offered with love for the betterment of the person and the relationship

To have a friend with whom you can share and discuss anything without recrimination or intimidation is an invaluable treasure. Having such a confidant allows one to verbalize thoughts which otherwise might cause stress and go round and round in the mind and never find a proper place to rest. Such a person can offer advice, and give encouragement and affirmations when needed. He or she becomes a reflecting wall and a strong wall of support in times of crisis. If you have such friends, hold on to them. They are worth their weight in gold. With gold at its present price those friends would be worth a fortune.

There is, of course, another side to all this. That is, how well do we know ourselves? Have you ever asked yourself, "Who am I and how do I fit in to the overall scheme of things around me?" Or "Am I here by accident or was it predestined that I should be here for a higher purpose?" If so, do I know what that higher purpose is? What do you think of yourself? How do you categorize yourself? Is the public you the same as the private you?

All these are fascinating questions to ask and answer. I think it is true that deep down we probably do know ourselves and who we really are. We know our thinking, our preferences, our attitudes, our hopes, our desires, and a myriad of parts which make up the whole.

Our responsibility is to ensure that the engine that drives all these aspects about us is well-oiled with a good attitude and healthy thinking, resulting in a natural expression of who we are. Hopefully it will display a person of compassion, kindness, and graciousness. We then live in hope that others will like what they see.

19.

Significance—Is It Important?

I would be amazed if significance is not high on your mental agenda. Whether you have thought about it or not. That is the way we are. None of us wants to feel insignificant. The strange thing with significance is that we need it for our mental well-being, yet we would be reluctant to readily admit that we feel significant. We would not want it interpreted as arrogance.

We all need a sense of being, a reason for being. We need a sense of purpose, of meaning and acceptance. We desire to be of importance, which comes partly from being needed. We want to make a difference. These aspects are all wrapped up in significance. Can we live without it? Probably, but it would not be pleasant and, in fact, could be quite depressing. Feeling insignificant is painful and it is not something that we like to acknowledge openly.

I am certain there are times when we all face such questions as, "Why am I here?" or, "Am I making a difference?" And the older we get we think, "What will I leave behind?" or, "How will I be remembered?" We might even wonder what might be said at our funeral (perhaps it might be better if we don't know). It is true, however, that our significance lives on after us. We are significant if we are making a contribution in our circle of influence. Remember, it is not always the loud and noisy who are significant, but the quiet, strong, and faithful. These provide deep and lasting significance.

We have friends who for years have given their time to serve at a food bank. They have made an invaluable contribution to those in need. I would call them significant people.

The critical issue here is that if significance is important to you and me then it is important to most people. So I am not dwelling here so much on our achievement of it but ask the question, "How often do we work at making each other feel significant?"

We might think it is just a question of making someone feel important. It is that but I think it is more than that. Surely the objective is for them to feel accepted by us. It is sad but true that some people try to be as they think we would like them to be. Our interest in them must always be genuine and authentic regardless of how they are. We should acknowledge them for the contribution they make to life and especially into our lives.

To make others feel significant we need openly to acknowledge who they are and what they have achieved in life. To recognize what they have accomplished as a father, a mother, an employee, or their value as a person in society. Where people have played a significant role, something good has always been achieved. They may have shown the right attitude or supported others who are less fortunate. There will always be aspects which should receive words of praise.

Think about this situation. It's just a simple illustration. A friend shares some exciting news—exciting to them even if not to us. How do we react? Do we respond positively and show a genuine interest in the conversation? Do we give it our full attention and not let our minds wander? Do we listen first and then reply? Do we find ourselves preparing our answer when we should be listening? Our response is critical. How we respond conveys to them the level of our sincerity and displays to them just how important they are, or not, to us.

Superficial and non-committal answers indicate our minds might be elsewhere and that the subject matter is of little significance to us. Because they identify very closely with their news, they will never feel significant if their news or conversation is summarily discarded. We need to respond with feeling and understanding. It is imperative that we recognize the conversation is not about us. It is all about them and what they want to share. The worst thing we can do is say, "Oh, yes, that reminds of when I…" Our mind should be totally focused on what is being said and what it means to them. There is no need for it to relate to an event in our lives. This is their news and we need to understand and appreciate that.

This is just one small way we can help others to enjoy significance—giving people our full attention, being interested in their lives, their joys, their disappointments and their struggles. It says to them that we value them and they are important enough for us to support them in life. By doing this we become assuring and affirming, and make a positive input into their lives. We are tacitly expressing our genuine friendship.

Why not go and make someone feel significant today?

20

The Scourge of Individualism

With a specific situation in mind, I asked a friend what he felt would drive a man to mistreat his wife after many years of marriage. His immediate answer was, "Individualism. It's all about me."

The conflict between individualism and collectivism has been a subject philosophers and students alike have discussed and dissected for many years, but that is not the premise of our discussion. We are not really looking at whether the needs of the individual are more important than society as a whole but how should we handle our interests and those of others with whom we interact? Individualism affects us all on a personal level, so how do we handle our personal freedom alongside the exercise of self-interest?

What is it that motivates someone to push in at the grocery check-out or to drive alongside your car in the closed lane and push in two cars ahead? The ten seconds saved seems more important to them than the consideration for others who also are in a hurry trying to get to work or to an appointment. How often do we see a dangerous driving maneuver in an attempt to get ahead, only to drive up alongside the car in question at the next traffic light? Road rage seems to be on the increase, and in some instances has resulted in "over the top" and inappropriate action. This too is instigated by the "me first" syndrome. No question that an "after you" attitude would reduce road rage enormously.

Are we so influenced by a self-centered society that we too jump on the "me" bandwagon? It is easy to do. Do we think of demanding our rights?

These same principles apply at work, at school, at church, or any other place where we mix with people. Do you remember the days when we would stand up and offer our seat to a lady on a bus? To hold a door open for others was normal. People seem amazed now if you go out of your way to be courteous. It is not uncommon today to get the door slammed in your face.

In business, this selfish attitude is often accompanied by manipulation and even deviousness to achieve the desired result. Work colleagues and friends are not impressed, just the opposite. You may think an "others first" policy leaves no room for assertiveness. That is not true. However, there is a line where assertiveness turns into aggression. You are not being a doormat by giving precedence to other people.

The "me first" attitude can invade our marriage. Individualism and self-centeredness in marriage can make for a miserable existence. It can bring isolation and disconnect. It creates suspicion. It damages and deteriorates the relationship. An immediate goal or desire might be achieved, but at what cost? At some point in the past we made a commitment and it was not "until I don't get my own way!" It was for better or worse. We are a team. We are made to be together.

So before we push our own agenda, inside or outside of marriage, we need to ask ourselves, am I helping or hindering the relationship concerned? What will be the ultimate result of my action? I am not a child but am I acting like a child? Is life really all about me?

I know we often think that life revolves around us, and in a sense it does, in that we are at the center of our own thinking. But life is more than us. It is true that we have the freedom to choose our beliefs, our lifestyle, and our actions, all of which are determined by our individual conscience. However, although we have certain rights to liberty and independence, others have those same rights. I once heard it said that, "Your freedom ends where my nose begins!" Putting that in reverse I would say, the exercise of my rights must end if my actions adversely affect you or the community at large. We need a balance between the two that hopefully provides a good result for both parties.

We need to be strong and not be influenced by the selfish attitude of our society. We do not have to look far to see utterly self-centered and selfish acts around us. But why not be different? If we act out of selfless and uncon- ditional love, hard as that may be, people will notice and it will bring its own lasting reward, especially since it not a common occurrence.

Oh yes, and by the way, talking about the checkout,

have you ever tried insisting someone else goes before you in the line? Try it. You might be pleasantly surprised at the response. You might make someone's day and you won't feel bad yourself!

21

You Have Only One Mind —Make the Most of It.

When you have done something idiotic or without thinking, people ask, "Where was your mind?" meaning, what were you thinking? Obviously not on what you were doing. However, if you were asked a different question, "Where is your mind?" what would you say?

Naturally your answer would be something like, "In my head," or "In my brain." Both of these answers could be correct but they do not pinpoint where your mind is in your brain.

I have read numerous books on the brain and can assure you there is no little box sitting in the middle of your brain of which you could say, "That contains my mind." It is common to have this image of one particular area that has stored up all our life memories, operates our mental faculties, and could possibly be labeled the mind or the control center. It seems that is not the case.

On occasions, surgeons have performed open-head brain surgery while the patient was awake. These primarily have been for diagnostic procedures for patients with serious epileptic problems. The interesting aspect has been, that when different parts of the brain have been probed, it has caused different memories to be recalled, with some parts of the same story coming from different parts of the brain. It is even thought that some of our recalled memories pick up various bits from different stories and put them together, so that even we believe the resulting tale to be true.

With the distribution of our mind in various places of the brain, you may very well be stating the truth when, on those odd occasions you might say, "My mind is all over the place!"

The brain is a complex organ that maintains our bodies, our actions, our thoughts, our memories, and our very life. Our bodies operate under constant instruction from the brain. Just like any other organ it can be attacked and damaged by injury or disease, and regrettably it is. These occurrences can be debilitating or even fatal.

The last few years have seen much discussion on keeping the brain active and well. Programs are available to do just that, both through the Internet and books. Most of us would benefit from a little brain exercise just as much as physical exercise. One aspect about the brain, however, is generally inferred and surmised, and I feel unjustly so. That is, that the brain automatically degenerates over time so that "the old" or "the elderly" are unfairly expected to show some evidence of mental incompetence. Maybe my age justifies, or at least motivates, my thinking.

There is medical proof that the brain gets smaller as

the years go by. There is also no question that a number of folks succumb to what once was commonly termed senility, which now seems to come under the umbrella of dementia. But that does not justify all of us who are passed retirement age being painted with the brush of *non-compos mentis*. Far from it. In fact, I read recently that only four percent of seniors suffer from serious dementia, while another ten percent experience a mild form of it. If we are talking only about memory loss, then that applies to any age group. We all have memories of faceless names and nameless faces regardless of our age. If you move location it is not long before people that you have known begin to fade into one of those categories.

From a survey taken, people under the age of 45 readily aligned senility or dementia with old age. In other words, older people are expected to slow down mentally, to be confused, become dependent, and possibly lose touch with reality. I would venture to say that is a question of misunderstanding. Sadly, that is what society teaches or at least implies by its expectations. If we, who are into those senior years, hold to that view, then it becomes a self-fulfilling prophecy. We expect it therefore it is. I honestly believe it does not have to be that way.

Many people have made great achievements in later life, like Verdi, composing opera in his seventies. I read about an author who started writing at age 75 and published five books before he died at 90. P. G. Wodehouse was 93 when he was working on his 97th novel. He died that year. Harry Bernstein published his first book, *The Invisible Wall*, at age 96. Helen Taussig, an American biologist, carried on her work even after moving to a retirement home. Every day she would go to her place of work and continue her research right up to the day she died in a car accident, three days before her 88th birthday.

Age is just a number. Mental decline is not inevitable. Your mind is what you make of it. We use it or lose it. So, folks, please don't ever send yourself off to the dump. I am certain you have much more to offer this world.

22.

Love Comes in Different Packages

*L*ove, such a small word but probably the most used word around the world. The subject is almost certainly the most popular. Think of the hundreds of thousands of books published annually, a high proportion of which would be romance novels. With non-fiction books and films also covering the subject, the word love is no stranger to any of us. It never has been. For centuries, it has been the subject of literature, plays, songs and operas. Romeo and Juliet comes readily to mind.

But love comes in many shapes and sizes. We have love for people, love for animals, love for hobbies, love for sports, and love for food, and so it goes on. So what distinguishes love from like? Although the word *love* would be used for some of the subjects mentioned, we would replace *love* with *like* for others. When we like something, we find it enjoyable or preferable over something else, whereas love is a deep affection for something or someone even to the point of passion.

Devotion to something can be driven by a love or a

like. We can even have a passion for a cause or a project. Dogs have been known, because of their devotion, to stay stoically by their owner who has fallen. Is that love or just faithfulness to an honorable provider and friend? There are many different aspects to this subject.

Tragically in some areas of life, love has been degraded and is equated with lust. In those cases love has just become a convenient word to use and has nothing in common with the real meaning; it is just a synonym for lust.

"Love makes the world go round"—so says an old song. Not sure about the practical truth of that but the sentiment is understood. Can you imagine a world without love? It would not make for a pleasant existence. Maybe love is an invisible glue that creates a certain stability in society. Whatever we think about that, love is a huge subject with so many different angles. In a book of quotations, I find almost three hundred entries on love, more than any other subject.

Can love be measured? Is it possible to have a superficial love? In comparison, what is unconditional love? I think our definition would be that there is no cost or price too high to pay for the establishment, existence, and continuation of a relationship. We wonder how many marriages have seemingly started out that way only for the unconditional aspect to fade away with time.

Love is of immense importance in life and in our lives. We all need to know that we are accepted and loved. Love brings happiness, contentment, and confidence. It creates security in the one made to feel loved. But none of this happens without the expression of love. I have wondered whether love is love if it is not expressed. If it is not expressed then where is it, in the heart, in the mind? But does it really exist until it is known by the object of the love?

I think the words of a song by Oscar Hammerstein II fit in well here.

> A bell's not a bell 'til you ring it
> A song's not a song 'til you sing it
> Love in your heart wasn't put there to stay
> Love isn't love 'til you give it away.

The outward expression of love is powerful. It carries an extreme positive emotional effect upon the recipient. It comforts, brings strength, consolidates relationships, and establishes new ones. Yet how reluctant we are to utter those three little words, "I love you!" If "I'm sorry" are the hardest words to say, then "I love you" should be the easiest, but that does not seem to be the case. Maybe self-consciousness or embarrassment are the culprits that deny us the freedom to use such an expression.

We need to love while we can and express it while we have the chance. Life brings twists and turns suddenly and often allows us no time to do those things that are in the back of our minds to do tomorrow.

Emigrating thousands of miles from home has its downside. My mother was rushed to hospital and because my father was 94 years old the authorities placed him in a home close by, to be cared for, for the duration of the hospital stay. In the home my father contracted a nasty virus and was moved to the hospital, where he died a few days later. My mother never got to see him. We never got to see him, either. There were no goodbyes. My mother recovered only to die a few months later. All this to say we need to express our love to those we love while we have the opportunity.

What a privilege to have family and others around whom we love! Let's take time to express those sentiments to them. We cannot tell them too often how much we love and care for them. Don't wait for a better or more convenient time. We may not be given the time. It is hard to live with a regret that we could have avoided with a little thought.

23.

The Quiet Epidemic

A serious malady of our present society is acute loneliness. Unheralded, yet it is thought to be of epidemic proportions. It is not something that people readily or quickly acknowledge but all age brackets are affected. Elderly people who have lost spouses rank high in the percentage count, but even among the 25 to 34 age group at least 25% admit to bouts of loneliness. A sense of disconnection, feeling unloved and unneeded—all contribute to the feeling of not fitting in or being left out.

It is ironic that over 50% of the population around the world now live in urban environments, so we are closer together, yet farther apart. We wonder how many high-rise apartments are filled with socially starved people. Sadly, we can be lonely in a crowd. Connecting and talking with one another has never been easier and so available, yet loneliness is still prominent. We have never been more connected, yet we are more distant. Why is that?

One contributing factor is the Internet. Remember when it was questioned as to why every home would even need a computer? Now it is not easy to find a home without one. Many people "surf the net," which absorbs many hours, usually spent alone. Others spend long periods of time on video games. Then come other communication devices that demand constant, and usually, instant attention. In fact, some people have a closer relationship with their mobile devices than with other people.

Unfortunately, what should be for our betterment and convenience has become a cause of separation. Technology is causing self-inflicted isolation. One day I was driving past a bus stop close to a school. There were 10 or 12 students in a line waiting for the bus. It was extraordinary to see that none of them was talking to each other. They all had their heads down looking at their tech devices. They were totally unaware of what or who was around them. They were choosing not to communicate. This self-imposed isolation goes on day after day. I am sure you have seen it in coffee shops, in stores, on buses, in fact anywhere people gather they are found to be more engaged in their private conversations or games, as opposed to social interaction.

Another cause of disconnection has come about from the demands of careers and employment. Constant pressure to succeed. Constant upgraded targets to achieve. Greater loads. Longer expected hours in the office. Free time is used to relax and recover. For many it has become necessary to move away from home and move to the big city. Consequently, the sense of belonging has disappeared. Family ties have been broken or weakened. People rarely stay in their family clusters any more. One writer has said that families are now scattered like confetti and loneliness is the result. People no longer identify with their roots.

Suicide has often been attributed to loneliness which is so emotionally damaging and carries many adverse physical consequences. It is understood to suppress the immune system and has an adverse effect upon the cardiovascular system. It creates stress and can cause sleeplessness. In his book entitled *Loneliness*, John Cacioppo talks about the physiological damage caused by the effects of loneliness, and states that it "may be hastening millions of people to an early grave." It is that serious. Loneliness takes people down some very nasty physical and mental paths as they search to counteract the terrible sense of abandonment.

Loneliness is different from solitude. Paul Tillich once said, "Loneliness expresses the pain of being alone and solitude expresses the glory of being alone." We are all different. For some, being alone brings pain. For others, it brings joy. Being alone is not the same as being lonely. I like to think that I am a social being but I also enjoy time spent alone. For the truly lonely it can be a nightmare.

If you are lonely what can be done? I don't think others can determine for you the way to go. Taking counsel is wise, especially if your loneliness is causing extreme stress. You must decide what is best for you. You need to be proactive and use initiative, going out of your way to become involved with people. Discover church groups or other groups of interest to you. Go to concerts. Where there are people there are potential friends. Consider an evening class or two. Maybe learn a new language.

Why not join the 72% of the population who belong to a small group of some kind? The purpose of the group can be recreational. It can even be related to an addiction or a specific illness or disease. Common interest binds people together. It might be an investment club, a coin collectors club or a motorcycle club. Perhaps join a gym. Many belong to these groups for the social aspect rather than the group's reason for being. We are social creatures and we need one another.

Cultivate friendships as you can. I understand it is not easy for the lonely who may have become withdrawn. Don't go overboard. Spend time listening to people and being genuinely interested in them. That builds friendships fast. Invest time and effort into people. The dividends produced are enormous and long lasting and will have a positive effect upon your loneliness.

24

Is Discipline a Nasty Word?

I think it is true to say that few of us like the word *discipline*. It conjures up for us ideas of "toeing the line" or of having to do something we did not want to do. We usually equate it with punishment. It works both ways. We exercise discipline or we receive discipline. But what kind of a world would we have without any discipline? If we equate discipline with law and order in this setting, then without it we would have anarchy, and nobody relishes that scenario.

When I was in the British Army, many years ago, I learned the meaning of discipline. From day one we were expected to obey and respect superior officers, as well as keep the rules and regulations of the Army. Not to do so invited the wrath of those in charge. Wrongdoing was met with punishment. I am not sure what they had done wrong but I remember spending a whole evening with a couple of friends who had to peel potatoes taken from a pile which was taller than they were.

But was it all bad? I think not, regardless of what I thought at the time. In fact, to be disciplined produced a very ordered life, but with it came self-esteem and a sense of well-being. It taught us self-discipline. It showed us that there was a world outside of ourselves that demanded our respect and attention. To ignore that was to our detriment. I believe that self-discipline, self-esteem, and self-respect are closely linked. They support each other.

Remember the days when parents would say to their children, "This is going to hurt me more than you" as they meted out punishment? As a child I could never understand that phrase. Parents discipline their children—why? It is not just to make them fall in line with the parental wishes. It is to make them better people. They want their children to respect others and be respected themselves. Standards and levels of acceptance are learned through discipline.

From the day we are born to the day we die we are learning. Yes, we acquire the knowledge of facts, but more than that, we also learn what is permissible—essentially right from wrong. Life is more than about us. It involves others around us. We learn that we cannot always demand or have what we would want in life. Many people have found out the hard way. That is why our prisons are full.

Sometimes we are called to exercise self-discipline to walk down the right road, and it's not always easy. The road we would choose might be good for us but not necessarily the best for our family. Our desires and feelings are overwhelming as we see an incredible opportunity and would wish to go down that road. It takes all the discipline in the world to choose to do the right thing, but choose we must and often for the sake of others.

Discipline is using reason to determine the best action for all concerned. Then the decisions made are usually sensible, informed, rational, and positive. For what it's worth, it is good also to know that self-discipline builds character.

You may be at a crossroad right now. One road appears to provide everything you desire, but there is another road that seems less attractive, and in your heart you know that is the road you must take. This is where self-discipline takes over. Let me encourage you; take the right road.

The extraordinary thing is that self-discipline brings freedom. It allows you to be the person you want to be within the parameters of the new circumstances. Once you are down that road you experience a great sense of contentment and satisfaction, having made the right decision. You are glad that you did what you knew you had to do. It confirms in your heart that you are in control. Life often will present us with a choice—exercise discipline or perhaps be disciplined. The former is better than the latter.

Discipline is not such a nasty word. Surprisingly it has our best interest at heart.

25

Is Kindness Contagious?

A video going around on Facebook showed people doing small acts of kindness or thoughtfulness. The predominant comments were along the lines of, "If only there was more of this, the world would be a better place to live in." I am sure we all concur with that thinking. Being kind according to the dictionary is being friendly, generous, or showing benevolence. It often involves affection, warmth, a gentleness, and a genuine concern for others. We also consider people to be kind by their manner, their kindly attitude, their helpfulness, their empathy, and their understanding.

Kindness is an attitude that results in kind action. It can be a simple action of a smile, or the recognition of anyone who provides you with a service, such as a sales person, a waiter, a police officer, or others with whom you have a passing contact. Telling people they are doing a good job, especially when their task appears to be so trivial or demeaning is also an act of kindness. Have you ever told the lady cleaning the tables in the coffee shop what a good job she is doing?

Kindness is also an act of encouragement. We were

surprised once when a neighbor called and said that she wanted to cook dinner for us. Who were we to refuse? Sure enough, her husband came around with chicken and rice and vegetables. It was wonderful and a great delight to us. She just wanted to bless someone and that she did. Shortly after that I was at the cash register of our local supermarket when the person ahead of me ran out of money to pay for her purchases. I offered the difference. It was less than 50c but by the reaction one would have thought it was $50. Such was the response. It was a very small act, but obviously a great encouragement.

A similar happening occurred at a discount store where I decided to pay for the purchases of the lady behind me. It was only $6.00, but again you would have thought it was $600. I received two hugs and continuous thanks all the way to my car. As I joined my wife in the car it was quite pleasing to tell her as I pointed out the lady in question, "That lady just gave me a hug!"

Kindness is a matter of the will. We should be willing to respond in kindness even when it is inconvenient, or perhaps even in situations with which we are not quite comfortable. Kindness means going the extra mile. J. R. R. Tolkien said, "Some believe it is only great power that can hold evil in check, but it is not what I have found. It is the small everyday deeds of ordinary folk that keep the darkness at bay by small acts of kindness and love." Kindness is being sensitive to the needs of others and then seeking to do something practical to meet those needs. The needs of people are varied and we need to be sensitive to situations they face. They may have a practical physical need that could readily be met. They may have an emotional need that may require much understanding, patience, and even some counseling to help bring about a solution.

Many years ago we received a telephone call from friends in England. Friends of theirs—a mother and daughter—were in trouble. They were on a visit to Canada and apparently were being treated intolerably by the people with whom they were staying. We were asked if we could help. My wife and I drove the fifty miles to find these people, extricated them from their situation, gave them accommodation, and cared for them until it was time for them to return to England. Years later Christmas cards still remind us of that much-appreciated event.

Humanly speaking we sometimes find it difficult to express kindness. It means overcoming self-consciousness. It means purposely forgetting our self-centeredness. We are naturally prone to be concerned with our own problems and situations. We do not automatically think of others first and their situations. It takes effort deliberately to choose to respond to someone else's need.

There are numerous stories of strangers stepping up with an act of kindness to fill a need and perhaps be the answer to someone's prayer. Kindness is like an ointment on an injury, it soothes and can take away emotional pain. I read how many celebrities have quietly come to the aid of those who have needed medical treatment. Without fanfare, they have put young people through college and set them on their way to complete their education. Some while ago someone organized "A day of random kindness" I think we need to instigate that again and again. Go out today and see who needs a little help. Buy someone a coffee or offer to buy a meal for a homeless person. Surprise someone. Do something unexpected. It will go a long way to encourage and lift people up. Why not be the one to set off a wave of kindness?

I asked the question, "Is kindness contagious? Absolutely. It has a ripple effect. How many times have you heard about someone buying coffee at the drive-through for the person in the vehicle behind? What is the result? That person invariably then buys for the next person behind them. As Sophocles is thought once to have said, "Kindness begets kindness!" Even more significant is a quotation by Tolstoy, "Nothing can make our lives, or the lives of others, more beautiful than perpetual kindness." If a small kindness can make such a huge difference in a person's life, then I would like to know that I have made someone's life beautiful. I am sure you feel the same way.

26

The Dark Prison of Depression

W hen we heard of a friend who had been released from her depression, we were delighted for her. I used the word *released* because that it is exactly what it is like. It's a very dark prison.

My wife, Rita, has experienced several bouts of deep depression over the years and we know the scenario well and all that it implies. The very word brings back memories we would rather forget. For some it begins with the gradual rolling in of dark clouds, bringing a sinister blanket of oppression and gloom. For others, including my wife, it can happen overnight or in the space of a few hours at any time. It can be triggered by a traumatic event or even on hearing some disturbing news, usually with a personal emotional application.

None of us is immune from depression. It matters not our profession—teachers, ministers, celebrities, and even doctors. All are known to have fallen prey to this nasty illness. The cause is varied but often related to the loss of a spouse, of a job, of home, a serious illness, divorce, or other trauma-inducing event. It is estimated that ten percent of the population will suffer at some point in their lives with a serious depressive disorder. Unfortunately, not all people seek medical help because of self-consciousness and embarrassment, because it is considered mental illness. The stigma over depression is horrendous.

Once depression arrives it brings with it a sense of helplessness. It takes over. Its demands are unrelenting for both sufferer and caregiver. Days upon days are spent with the air of despondency, of constant crying, and hours of motionless sitting. Someone described it as a long dark tunnel with no light at the end. You are even imprisoned in your own house. There comes an aversion to meeting people and an inability to deal with normal everyday activity. Sometimes comforting arms are all that one can give.

Depression is unpredictable as to how long it will last. Rita's episodes were usually four months long. Few people can comprehend four months of emotional darkness. Four months living with a sense of hopelessness. It is not surprising that it brings a desire to end one's life. For the caregiver it brings on a sense of inadequacy in dealing with the situation. Occasionally, for me to leave the room caused my wife great consternation.

Our friend's recovery reminded me again of how grateful we are that it has been almost ten years since Rita suffered her last insidious bout with depression. Unless you have been there, it is difficult to fully understand the devastation it brings, especially a sense of failure.

How do you beat it? How do you overcome it? A

personal faith helps, although even there it can be accompanied by a sense of guilt. Guilt that this kind of thing should not happen if you are a Christian. Often inferred is a lack of faith in God, which could not be further from the truth. Sadly, many people in the church do not understand depression. Once when Rita was on the road to recovery we returned to church, where she was greeted with, "Why don't you snap out of it?" If it were that simple why would anyone remain in a self-inflicted prison? It is not an illness of choice. People suffering with depression need love, comfort, understanding, and support—not criticism!

Yes, many drugs are used, but sometimes even they are hit-and-miss in determining the right one and the right dosage. There is no simple formula. Doctors are quick to prescribe antidepressants. They are trained to treat the symptoms and not look for the cause. Causes vary but often are related to a stress factor. How we handle worry and stress will invariably determine the onset, or not, of depression. Generally, the cause has long passed and the clock cannot be reset. However, I have read that our thoughts and attitude in the present can provide a very positive response to just such a dark situation, even to the possibility of reversing the ill effects of depression and keeping future attacks at bay. I spent many hours just holding my wife, talking, praying, reading Scripture to her, and looking for the glimmer of improvement.

The whole scenario is like walking through a very dark forest. The trees are dense and block out the sunlight. The forest seems endless. The blackness is almost tangible. Then one day there appears just a slight fleeting ray of sunlight. A few days later another and then another until through a gap in the trees you see the sunshine on the side of the mountain. You have reached the other side of the valley. You walk out of the forest into the warmth of the sunlight.

Then you know it is finally over and everything is fresh and new again. Your strength returns and you realize the joy of climbing towards the next mountaintop experience.

27

The Magic of Memories

Have you ever heard a piece of music and immediately you are transported elsewhere? The time and place has changed and you are back into the familiar surroundings associated with the music.

It happens to me when I hear certain music from the sixties—which is not too often now—but immediately I am taken back into the army barracks. It is afternoon and the sun is shining through the windows. I am walking down the center of the room between the two rows of beds. I sense the smell of the barracks. Although conscripted into the army and not there out of choice, the music still brings back a certain element of nostalgia. I am sure you have experienced something quite similar.

The mind is incredible. It stores so many memories for us; some new, some old, some good, some bad. We tend to repress the bad, those we would prefer not to dig up again. Unfortunately, they are still there however much we like to have them forgotten. It is thought that all that happens to us in life is stored somewhere in the brain—quite a thought.

Through our memories, the mind can whisk us back

into time and across continents in a split second. Quite unexpectedly things that happen in the present bring memories to the surface, some which have been buried for years, while others are more recent. Photos are important as reminders of days gone past. They usually record the good times or the celebratory occasions. Photos are irreplaceable. Refugees try to take photos with them when forced from their homes. Family photos lost in a fire cause much sadness.

It is often the small things that trigger the recollection of past events. You remember the looks, the words spoken and meaningful touches. They seem to be as vivid today as on the day they occurred. You read an article, you see someone or hear something spoken, and the memories flood back. The amazing aspect is that the mind brings back the thoughts and the feelings you were having at the time the event took place. It affects you in the present. If you were happy, then it is pleasing. If you were sad, then it makes you feel unhappy. It may be the passing of a loved one or a good friend. Your memories of them return and you refresh and enjoy again those special moments you had with them.

I allude to this in another chapter but I find it fascinating. Neuroscientists tell us that not all memories are totally true. Because the brain stores different aspects of the same memory in different places, it sometimes puts together pieces of more than one similar experience and we recall the memory in that way. We relate the story as though that is how it happened. Yet the mind has done a little embellishing of the story without our knowledge.

I find that a little disconcerting. It makes me wonder if I am sharing falsified memories. I will never know. Anyway, I will not lose any sleep over it. If you ask me about my childhood memories I will still tell you the same stories.

Not all memories bring back happiness and joy. Deprived are those people whose remembrances bring only further sadness because of hurts and struggles. They remember the discord and conflict in a dysfunctional family setting. Memories are but thoughts and fortunately, in this instance, they fade as time passes.

However. I am sure that most of us have fond memories that arise again and again. Every time I hear the singing of a male voice choir, immediately I am returned to earlier days of singing in a mass men's choir in the Royal Albert Hall and in the Royal Festival Hall in London, England. The euphoric sensation is just as strong as it was then. The elation returns as one relives the memory.

Take care of your good memories. Recall them. Enjoy them. A friend said that her mother was always laughing and that's the memory she treasures. Someone referred to the memory as a mental scrapbook, which is a good analogy. In your scrapbook you may have pictures of washing the grazed knee of your child, drying the eyes over the dropping of an ice cream, reading a bedtime story or opening a special Christmas gift. All are small vignettes of your past etched in the mind, which bring back the nostalgia or pleasure of that moment. The hurricane of life might take away our surface possessions but it can never wipe out our precious memories.

We are making new memories all the time. It is

important that we consciously do that. So go to places you have not been before. Do things that are out of your comfort zone. Do those things that you have always put off until a better time. Maybe now is the time. Check out your "to do" wish list and see what is still to be done. Spend time with your family, your children, or your grandchildren.

Your family is special. Give them some special memories to store in their memory bank. One day when you are not around it could be important to them, as they may want to make a withdrawal from the bank!

This Business of Dying

I sat having a coffee with a friend in McDonalds. He shocked me with the news that he had cancer of the liver and was given five to eleven months to live. He had refused chemotherapy as he felt it would diminish the quality of life he had left. He appeared to be coming to terms with his situation and even talked about his funeral. I wondered how I would be under those circumstances.

Two days later he was in hospital. His cancer had spread considerably. He was given four to six weeks to live. In fact, he died 12 days after our coffee together. Fortunately, I was able to visit him the day before he died. The speed at which this all took place is mind-blowing. The family must have found it unbelievable and hard to grasp.

As friends, how do we handle this kind of situation? How does the family handle such a devastatingly rapid decline in the health of their loved one, followed by death? Even when expected the finality of death is hard to accept. If it is a shock to us, what is it to the family? There are no easy answers and it can seem trite to say that time heals, even if we know it usually does. I realize that this is not an unusual occurrence but one that we might be forced to face at some point in our lives.

The reality is that none of us, either as individuals or families, is immune to such a devastating event. It could happen to any one of us, at any time. The question that comes to mind is, "How would we deal with it, if such a thing suddenly came upon us?" I think it is virtually impossible to say how we would react. The event is not before us at this moment, so we don't have to deal with it. But it certainly causes us to face the possibility.

The last time I checked the ratio of dying was, and always has been, 100%. So we all, maybe reluctantly, have to face our own mortality and that of our family members, however hard that may be. Our age is no guarantee that we have a certain amount of time left. My friend was four years younger than I, which adds a stark reality to it.

One comment I heard was that we need to live every day as though it were our last, but the person also said, "How many of us do that?" Practically speaking, I think that is difficult to do. We are not going to run around and make sure we talk to those with whom we would want to have said goodbye. However, we know what the statement means. It is simply a reminder that we only have a certain number of days and we need to make the most of them. We don't need sermons to tell us what we should do, but just encouragement to make a difference while we have the time.

Here's a stark question of reality. What would we do if this were our last week? Have we said all the things we would like to say to our spouse and friends? Have we put things right which should never have caused division in the first place? Have we done the things we have always wanted to do to show we cared? Will we leave behind the remembrance of an attitude that will be missed?

At such a time, I guess it comes down to what is important. My friend had been a successful business-man. He had owned a thriving commercial enterprise and several properties, but all that held little significance. At a time like that our bank account and what we own become meaningless. The positions we have held are no longer important. It is what we leave behind that will continue to make a difference. The love we have shown. The lives we have touched. This is what people will remember. It may seem all very sobering but it's worthy of our thinking,

On a lighter note, while thinking about this business of dying, I am always reminded of a humorous quotation which has several versions. I shall use this one. "I don't mind dying, I just don't want to be around when it happens!" Unfortunately, we don't have an option.

29

What Will Be Your Legacy?

When I was in the business world I heard it said, "I don't plan to leave a legacy. I have taught my children how to fend for themselves!" I guess those people live by the adage of the bumper sticker that says, "Live long enough to spend your children's inheritance!" So I assume for those same people this chapter will fall on deaf ears. However, for the rest, let me ask this question.

Do you ever think about the legacy you plan to leave? At some point or other in life most of us think about a legacy. We either live in the hope of receiving one or we think of the legacy we might leave. I believe we would all like to leave a mark on the wall of life to say, "I was here." It would be good to say, "This is what I contributed to life and this is what I am leaving behind."

A life well lived should leave a good legacy, but what testifies to a life well lived? Some believe that if you have traveled around the world and seen all there is to see, then you have arrived and lived a full life. Others think that rising through the ranks into a prestigious position of power and influence is the ultimate. Still others believe that acquiring wealth and possessions is the height of freedom and achievement. I'm sure you've heard the common saying, "He who finishes with the most toys, wins." This leads me to ask the question, "If all these positions and possessions were achieved, what is left behind to say the person made a difference while they were here?" All the toys are left but what do they say?

Although not having read it myself, I found an interesting quotation on legacy from John Nichols' book *The Nirvana Blues*. He said, "Each person leaves a legacy – a single, small piece of himself, which makes richer each individual life and the collective life of humanity as a whole." A principle that we would all like to achieve; something of ourselves which makes others richer because we were here.

I once read, "When we are dead we are all equally dead." Obviously true, but I like the emphasis upon the word "equally." We are equal when we arrive because we arrive with nothing, and when we leave, we leave with nothing. We are all born equal with the prospect of life before us and all that it holds. Likewise, we are equal at the end of life's journey. What happens in between is crucial for what we leave behind.

Perhaps you heard about the man who wanted to take his money with him. During his life he had been rather mean to his wife and miserly with his money. He demanded his wife bury his money with him. To this she agreed. When he died she dutifully wrote a check and placed it in the coffin.

Sadly, legacies can be the cause of much bitterness

and conflict within families, but they can also be a pleasant surprise for others. But there is more to a legacy than just the passing on of monetary gifts and possessions.

Will you be leaving a rich legacy of who you are? Will it be for what you have achieved or will it be for the example you have been? It usually is one of those. If your life were to be summed up in a story, what story would it tell? When your children or grandchildren think of you, will they immediately remember about the love and kindness you had for them and for others? Will they remember the life principles by which you lived?

Many of us do not have much by way of wealth to leave but that does not exclude us from leaving a rich inheritance. I came to the conclusion that the only way to make a difference and leave your mark is by investing your time, energy and efforts into the lives of other people now. By making a positive change in someone's life you leave an indelible mark. They will know you have passed this way. By showing love, respect and giving support in times of crises, others will know you cared for them. That leaves a lasting legacy which has no comparison.

Life is short. Our time is limited. We need to work at living a life now which reflects honorable principles where others come first. Live to be missed. Live a life by which you want to be remembered. That way your legacy will be invaluable and unsurpassed to those left behind.

30

Forgiven

orgiveness has one of the most powerful effects upon our human psyche, both from the giving and receiving of it. To give it is to be released from a prison of anger and resentment. To receive it is to be released from underlying animosity and guilt for being the cause of the rift.

Giving and receiving forgiveness are two sides of the same coin. A lack of forgiveness brings with it untold stress, which in turn causes innumerable adverse medical conditions. Research studies have shown that approximately 80% of illnesses are mind related. Our mental activity has an enormous direct relation to the physical. It has been discovered that high blood pressure, heart attacks, anxiety, depression, stomach problems, headaches, and sleeplessness can all be birthed in un-forgiveness, and the resentment and bitterness it causes. A lack of forgiveness is known to cause mental illness.

One of the best books I have read on the subject is *None of these Diseases,* by Dr. S. I. McMillen. He so ably relates the link between the mind and the body. He outlines how it is that different parts of the anatomy are affected by different forms of mental stress, such as anxiety and guilt. The colon seems to be a favorite for reacting to stress and worry. Guilt increases the heart rate and blood pressure, both of which have an adverse effect upon the cardiovascular system.

Fortunately, forgiveness has the opposite effect and can reverse the unwanted medical symptoms mentioned above. By withholding forgiveness we do more damage to ourselves than the person who is waiting for forgiveness. The person who caused us the hurt can do no more than ask for forgiveness, and is then forced to move on with life while we continue to hang on to the hurt and allow it to grow unnecessarily larger in the mind, resulting in resentment and a distasteful feeling against the adversary, which they have now become.

We all have experienced times when we see the situation differently from someone else. We are reluctant to compromise by moving away from our position. The other person does the same, so rather than agreeing to differ and keeping the peace, we hold our ground because we are right. Sometimes harsh words are spoken, which results in damaging a good relationship. Both parties leave sad, disillusioned, and nursing a hurt which only forgiveness from both sides will heal. Unfortunately, this unresolved situation can continue for months and even years. It is the perfect scenario for one to get sick. The only resolution is the conscious letting go of negative emotions, offering the olive branch of forgiveness, which leads to reconciliation and a repaired relationship.

When we take an honest look at our hurts they pale

into insignificance when we think about the atrocities that have occurred against others. When we read of parents who have forgiven those who have murdered their child, we are astounded and find it difficult to understand. We wonder how that could be done. It can only be done through the incredible power of love. In such a situation, we ask who benefits. It is those who let go of the hurt. They are released from their incessant pain. That is an extreme and extraordinary act of forgiveness but it demonstrates how hurts of a lesser nature can more easily be put to rights.

Another aspect of forgiveness is forgiving ourselves. Being human, we make mistakes, sometimes with devastating results. How many times have we wished to go back in time to undo the things we may have done thoughtlessly or carelessly? People have moved away or passed on and how we wish to have the opportunity again to say "sorry," but it is no longer available. How do we deal with that? We genuinely offer forgiveness from our heart and mind and maybe even write it out on paper so that it is a tangible and practical act. We can then be free to forgive ourselves and move on with life.

However difficult it is, for the sake of our health, we have to learn to forgive and also to receive forgiveness. It just takes one person to act humbly and make the move towards resolving the issue. However hard it might be, the end result is worth it. I have heard it said that the two words in the English language hardest to say are, "I'm sorry!"

The freedom of forgiveness, in both giving and

receiving, is unsurpassed. Forgiven! What a wonderful word but even better is the experience.

31

What Is Your Biggest Regret in Life?

If I were to ask you, "What is your biggest regret in life?" what might your answer be? Maybe you have no regrets. If so, you are very fortunate and probably in the minority. When faced with the same question others have said their regrets include putting work over family, not having the confidence to put forward their point of view, not completing their education, not taking care of their health, and being subject to other people's opinions. The list goes on.

So go back to the question for a moment and think how it might apply to you. It might surprise you what comes to mind. Some regrets are hard to live with because of their depth of cause and effect. Others are easier to handle because they might be superficial and have made little difference to your life. Many regrets bring with them a sense of extreme frustration because of the inability to go back and put them right.

If you could turn the clock back what would you change? If you could choose to make things different from what they are now, how different would your life be? We would all like to eradicate the memories of events that have left scars and brought hurt to our families. But how would you change your present life? Would you have a different job or profession, a different home in a different location, or maybe different friends? Unfortunately, we don't get a practice run at life, it's the real thing from the beginning. We are where we are because of choices made by us or other people.

As I get older I can't help looking back and reflecting on what has been. If I had known years ago what I know now, would I have taken a different road? To be honest, I am not sure. What I have done has been good, rewarding, and very satisfying, but I wonder if there might have been something else whereby my life would have made an equal or better contribution to those around me. I suppose most of us think that we might have achieved something more than we have. It may not have been the case but we like to think so.

When I was 15 years old I wanted to go to the Royal College of Music in London and become an orchestral conductor. I now think, "How absurd!" My total musical ability at that time was an ability to sing and play the recorder!! (Don't laugh too hard.)

Naturally, that particular unfulfilled desire does not bring any regrets, but other aspects of my life do. Things that were thoughtlessly said, things done that were unwise, things left undone that should and could have been carried out. Choices play an integral part when we begin to think of regrets. Bad choices naturally bring regrets. How often do we wish that we might have taken the other fork in the road? How often do we look back and perhaps wish we had chosen another option?

A nurse at a palliative care facility noted end of life regrets from some of her patients. None were surprising. No one said, "I wish I had spent more time at the office!" It was just the opposite; "I wish I had not worked so hard but had been home for my children's sports events," or, "I wish I had given more time and attention to my wife and family." "Why did I think that business trip was more important than my son's graduation?" Then there were more inward regrets like, "I wish I had loved more and expressed that to those for whom I cared." Another one said, "I wish I had been more honest with myself and open with others." One person said, "I wish I had taken my faith more seriously!"

Other people's actions can cause us regret and that is a difficult one to handle, because decisions by others are totally out of our control. We can only deal with decisions we have made earlier in life. I remember when we moved to Canada in 1964. There was someone to whom I knew I should go and say goodbye. In the busyness of the days prior to leaving I did not go. We returned for a visit two years later and the gentleman had passed away. It might seem a small thing but I have remembered it to this day because it was so impressed upon me to visit him and I didn't.

If we are honest, I am sure we all have regrets that come to mind occasionally, some small and insignificant while others loom large in our thinking. But what do we do with them? Unfortunately, we cannot turn back the pages of the calendar. We cannot always right the wrongs, bring back the spoken word, or offer help where it is no longer needed.

Rightly or wrongly, my solution is that we should acknowledge them, recognize the impossibility of changing the situation, and consciously put them aside. Holding on to regrets does not bring people back or heal relationships. If it is still possible to right a wrong then we should do so and get rid of one regret. The rest we have to accept that we made choices that perhaps were wrong. We made decisions that were mistakes. We have to admit that we were never perfect nor ever will be. The positive aspect of all this is that it teaches us to value what we have, the time we have left, and maybe give us the determination not to cause ourselves any more regrets.

Looking at a less serious regret let me say this. Some people have what is commonly called a bucket list of things they want to achieve in life, like skydiving or mountain climbing and all that kind of stuff. As for me, you can imagine what steps I am taking to avoid my ultimate potential regret, "I don't want to get to the end of my life and say, I wish I had enjoyed more apple pie and ice cream."

32

Have You Ever Been Exposed to Nerve Gas?

You might say, "If I had been exposed to nerve gas, I would not be here now," and you would most likely be right, although many people have survived, albeit with much suffering.

A nerve gas is used in chemical warfare. It is considered to be a weapon of mass destruction because of its ability to destroy thousands of people at one time. Knowing the devastating consequences, it is inconceivable how man can use it against his fellow man. Regrettably it happens, a move which one can only describe as evil. However, the weapon of mass destruction that I refer to is not used in chemical warfare, it is used in our everyday lives. If you can speak you use it. It is the tongue.

I am sure you have heard the debate about whether women speak more than men. I won't get into that discussion, but I believe it is not so much a gender issue as a difference in personality. Some people are quiet and reserved, so consequently they tend to speak less, while others who are more outgoing are prone to speak more. We have a friend who loves to talk. I am sure you do too, but what she says is always interesting. The important aspect is not in the number of words we use but how we use them.

If you are like me you probably know someone who has been destroyed because of a false rumor or others who have been irreparably hurt by a cutting tongue. It is a sad reality of life. A wrongful or spiteful accusation can destroy a career, a marriage, a family, or a life. We know a teacher who was falsely accused of misconduct by a student taking revenge for a low mark in class. It finished his teaching career even when there was no truth to the issue. The hurt is especially painful and the damage more severe when the false accusation is made in public. It is difficult to control public perception. People consider there is no smoke without a fire, but unfortunately, it would appear that with the tongue some people can create artificial smoke.

The tongue is a very small organ of the body but it can do much damage, and yet it can bring so much joy. By using it we can bring people down or we can build them up. With one false sentence we can destroy a life. We can encourage or discourage. We can bring a blessing or a curse. We can scatter gossip or bring comfort and healing. The tongue can be full of poison or it can be an instrument of love. We have the choice.

Can you imagine being instructed to cut open a pillow and allow all the feathers to fly freely into the air, then be asked to gather them all up and put them back inside the pillow? Obviously, it would be an impossible task. Someone suggested this illustrates the effect of gossiping or passing on a falsehood. The damage is beyond repair. The spoken word cannot be retrieved, it can never be brought back.

You may know this quotation from the book of Proverbs, "A word aptly spoken is like apples of gold in settings of silver." What a wonderful picture? It conveys the principle that the right word at the right time is priceless in what it can achieve. An appropriate word has the ability to reach inside and touch the heart.

It is within our control and power to bring a positive message to those who need it. We can make our words count for good. We can offer words of comfort in a grieving situation. We can speak words of peace into a conflict. We can seize the opportunities to build people up, to encourage them and help heal their brokenness through words of support. We can help lift them out of depressive states. With our tongues we have the capacity to touch people's lives for the better.

Let's accept a sense of responsibility and use our words to make a difference to those around us. There is a greater blessing in giving than receiving, and that applies to words too. Give some kind words away today. I am certain that someone who comes across your path today would be blown away by a few words of encouragement. Find something to compliment. Tell them what a good job they are doing. Tell them they look nice today. Such a small thing but so meaningful. Deliberately make the decision to offer some words of blessing. It will be the making of someone's day.

33

Have You Changed Your Mind?

I t used to be said that it was a woman's prerogative to change her mind. That may still stand, but today we are told that all of us can change our mind and in so doing change our brain.

If you have read *Switch on your Brain*, by Dr. Caroline Leaf—which I thoroughly recommend—you will quickly discover that our thinking is critically important. What we think and how we think effects the continual development of our brain. We learn that there is a distinction between our minds and our brain, they are not synonymous. The mind, where all the thoughts occur, gives instructions to the brain.

The old thinking was that the brain is fixed, could not change, and would automatically decline in efficiency as we age. That is no longer the understanding. While we feed our brain, it will continue to develop regardless of age. Every thought causes a chemical reaction in the brain with a positive or negative result. What a startling thought that is! Hence, we are constantly building our brains, for better or for worse.

The good aspect is that we are in charge and can

control the input into our minds. We control what we think. We have heard so many times that we are what we eat, but it seems more true to say, "we are what we think." Our thoughts create the foundation of our life, our actions, and our achievements. This statement is so true: "As a man thinks, so he is!"

I doubt whether we could ever totally comprehend how the billions of cells in the brain cooperate and achieve all that they do for us. From the daily functioning of our bodies to the comprehension and storing of information from reading and conversation. Over ninety percent of our actions originate from the non-conscious. Far more activity goes on there than in the conscious part of our brain. It indicates that our real self is probably more predicated upon our subconscious than we might imagine. Our actions are a direct result of our thoughts. Now we can begin to understand just how important and critical our thinking is.

Our principles for living and our belief system play an important part in who we are, how we think and what we do. Even if we cannot define our belief system, it still dictates our behavior because that is who we are. We act out what is inside us. What is in our mind determines the messages sent to the brain. The brain in turn sends messages to the body. Thus, the body becomes the expression of the mind. It really is mind over matter.

Some would theorize that the body, acting as the mind, dictates to the brain, while others suggest that the brain dictates to the mind. However, in both of those cases it would eliminate free will and we would be nothing but brain-controlled robots. All actions begin with our thinking. Everything hinges on the workings of the mind. We are not subservient to our brains but our brain is subservient to our mind.

Some people have had a serious accident and were told they would never walk again, but the mind is stronger than the body. A positive-minded person refuses to accept that outcome and determines to walk again. The mind conveys the desired vision to the brain which in turn instructs the body. So, with a positive attitude, discipline, and determination, they walk again, much to the amazement of the medical staff and their family. This concept makes good sense of the comment, "I think I could do that if I put my mind to it." That's the crux. We could probably achieve far more than we imagine if we put our minds to it. Maybe we downplay and underestimate what we are capable of achieving.

Neuroplasticity, the changing of the brain, has become a well-known fact over the last decade or so. It rewires the brain to perform functions previously lost. Stroke and accident victims have recovered with both physical and mental rehabilitation, being helped along by a positive mindset. The mind is powerful. It can bring about results either positive or negative, determined by the attitude. If one says, "I could never do that," it becomes self-fulfilling and it cannot be done.

One of the amazing aspects of medical treatment is the effect of the placebo. Numerous studies and anecdotes exist to testify to the positive results where people have been given a placebo or inert medication. It is a matter of belief. Those who believe that they are being given a new or powerful drug respond accordingly and often get well. It is similar to those who are told that, because of their particular intelligence and background, they will do well on a certain test—and they do. Others given the opposite information do badly. The mind is strong and determines more than we recognize.

The story is told of Natan Sharansky, formerly Anatoly Shcharansky, a Russian Jew who was a computer genius. He was jailed in the Soviet Union after being falsely accused of spying for the United States. He was given a nine-year sentence, 400 days of which were in solitary confinement. In his small, dark, cold, and dismal cell he needed to keep his sanity, so he mentally played chess against himself each day, keeping note in his mind of the positions of each piece on the board. After he was released from prison he emigrated to Israel where he eventually became an Israeli Cabinet Minister. In 1996 Gary Kasparov, the world chess champion, visited Israel and played a simultaneous match against 25 people. He beat all of them except Sharansky.

Knowing that the brain is ready to be changed it is up to us to change our mind. If we want more self-confidence we can obtain it. We must introduce it into our thinking. We can do the same for aspects in our lives that we want to lose. To keep the brain healthy and ever expanding we need to read, converse, discuss, learn something new, and do something different. We need to think good, positive thoughts that will instruct our brains accordingly. The effort will pay dividends. It will increase our enjoyment of life, create a positive attitude, and will help us make a valuable contribution to our life and the lives of those around us.

34

How Often Should We Eat Pumpkin Pie?

I love mince pies. Tragically, the bakeries seem to make them only at Christmas time. However, when it comes to pumpkin pie it seems now that it is served all the year round. I thought that was only a Thanksgiving thing but it seems it is no longer. It does, however, remind us of that time of the year and its accompanying theme. Are we really grateful for what we have in life? Yes, things could always be better, but then they could always be worse. Society pushes us to own. We are constantly encouraged to buy. We live in an age of "I want" or "I must have."

It is amazing how much we have come to believe we have a right to possess the newest gadgets and latest conveniences. We are egged on by advertising which insists that life would be intolerable without the products offered. Sadly, we often fall for that ploy. There is nothing wrong with possessions, and owning the nicest or latest of anything, but if we dwell too much on what we cannot own, it will blind us to the many blessings in life we can enjoy for which we can be grateful.

Thankfulness is something we choose. It begins in the heart when we begin to recognize how life might be without the provisions and the comforts of the present. When we think about the word *thanksgiving*, we are naturally reminded of the everyday provisions and all the pleasantries of our lives, such as our home, our safety, and the privilege of living where we do. Even if we are not well off, we are rich in comparison to those who have to live on $2.00 a day. I read that if we have a bank account and some money in our pocket, then we are among the top 8% of the world's wealthiest people. You may not feel that way but it simply highlights the vast majority who live in deprivation.

So where does our thankfulness begin? What about starting with the people in our lives? Do they not rank high in the order of our thankfulness? Spouses, of course, should be at the top of the list. How often do we thank them for who they are, for what they do, and the support they give? Maybe there has been sacrifice along the way that should be recognized. A card or note of appreciation goes a long way, allowing them to feel special for the day. A hug would also not be out of place. What about our children? Are they not worthy for us to express our gratitude for the part they play in our lives? Looking at things honestly, it may have been a struggle at times during their upbringing but the joy of having them around outweighs the downside of those difficult times.

Have you ever thought of writing a letter to your parents or even to your son or daughter, to express your gratefulness for who they are and for just being themselves?

Thinking of parents, eulogies are good in their place at funerals, but how much better to say those complimentary things while people are alive and can appreciate the sentiment. Think back to the good times of family vacations, special occasions of weddings, Christmas, and other family celebrations. Put the memories on paper and express how meaningful those experiences were. Such a letter to your parents would bring so much happiness and would be a joy to read.

Expressions of gratitude and thanks also bring their own rewards to us. It is difficult to be angry and grateful at the same time. It is difficult to be negative and thankful. Gratefulness is accompanied by a positive attitude. A person living in thankfulness tends to be upbeat and adds joy to the party. Such people become known by their pleasant and inspiring attitude. Isn't that how we like to be known?

So, we ask the question, how often should we eat pumpkin pie? I say all the year round if it reminds us of how grateful we are for all that we enjoy in life. Now if I could only get the bakeries to offer mince pies all the year round!

35

What Is Success?

Ninety-nine people out of a hundred would probably say that success is having sufficient financial independence to buy whatever you want to buy, to do whatever you want to do and when you want to do it. It provides a freedom without restrictions or boundaries. In other words, a world that provides all one could ever want. Many of us might envy such a position but it does not come without strings attached.

In the world of motivational speakers, the subject of success is foremost. Many times we have heard that reading such books as, *Think and Grow Rich*, *The One Minute Millionaire*, *Rich Dad Poor Dad*, and *Creating Wealth*, are critically important if we want to succeed. Reading such books, we are told, supports the adage that, "If you can think it, you can achieve it."

Now I am not out to dispute this statement, but it is somewhat discouraging for the many who read the books yet their lives did not change, their bank accounts did not fill up, and their lifestyle remains what it always has been, mediocre. There is no doubt that a positive attitude makes a world of difference to achievement and to the enjoyment of life, but when the goal of money and possessions is equated with the word *success*, many feel precisely the opposite. It instills a sense of failure. Whether that is true or not hinges upon one's concept of success.

Money alone does not bring success or satisfaction. Look at the millionaires, particularly those people in show business. Why have so many committed suicide? They had plenty of fame and money but obviously needed much more. Check out lottery winners. Many have come down with cancer, gone broke, or died, all within six months of receiving the payout. Money and possessions are not the key; these are just material things that hold very little long-term value and satisfaction.

You can lose all of these things in a split second. All the wonderful possessions we might own—like our house, our car, our collections, whatever we have—can be gone in a moment. Whether in a raging fire or sudden financial collapse, we can be left homeless and penniless. I read of a writer who sadly lost everything in a fire at his home. He lost his library, all his research, and the manuscripts on which he was working at the time. If our success is reliant upon things, and if they disappear, our success also disappears. Can we be successful while owning nothing?

Have you ever really sat down and thought about what you really want out of life? Do you really want success or is it the money you think success will bring? Is it the popularity which often accompanies success? Some people wish they could turn the clock back, because success for them has taken away their life—well, at least their personal and private life. Popularity is not all it is cracked up to be.

Is your conception of success vague? Have you ever tried to define it and how it would look in your life? We imagine that success is always determined by what we seek on the outside but maybe it has more to do with the pursuit and attainment of an inner sense of wellbeing that comes from a purposeful and meaningful life. Can we have success in life regardless of circumstance?

If you are frustrated that life does not seem to be providing the outward trappings of success for you, then maybe you are looking in the wrong place. There are principles in life already set out which provide the base for enjoying a life of success, not necessarily with overflowing bank accounts, but success nonetheless. It depends on how it is measured.

If material gain is the end objective then it goes no further. If, however, we look beyond that to a deeper, more meaningful concept of success, then we need to seriously consider some age-old principles of life such as diligence, discipline, conscientiousness, sincerity, determination and motivation. These principles have worked for others and they can work for you. If we are looking for practical success, then a faithful application of these disciplines will undoubtedly bring about positive results.

Most of us like to read stories of people who have made it from rags to riches. We admire people who have worked hard against all odds and created a successful life for themselves and their family. What has been their driving force? Determination, motivation, and hard work. That kind of success is open to all who will follow the same pattern.

But real success is more than that. You see, success is an attitude, a state of mind. And although outward circumstances can enhance positive feelings and contribute to the understanding we have of success, yet the situation alone does not intrinsically bring success. It is deeper than that. We can enjoy success in any environment. Millions of people enjoy a personal sense of success and fulfillment while not having much by way of possessions or money in the bank. Often, they will have menial jobs but are contented with their lot and are, in their own mind, successful.

When I asked my wife what her definition of success was, she gave a very simple answer. "Success," she said, "is achieving what you set out to do!" I like that. In fact, I think it is hard to beat that definition. It is a very wide and all-encompassing definition that can apply to all situations. What we might set out to do could be very simple to other people but success for us nonetheless. Whether it is to complete a project, learn a skill, fulfill a dream, take a lifetime trip, or get some education. Whatever it is, the completion of any one of these is a personal achievement and therefore successful.

Think about this. For some, learning to walk again or to talk again after a stroke would be success. For others, to find a long-lost family member would be a huge success. I am sure you can think of many other objectives others may have had which might be small achievements to us, yet life-changing for them.

So success is what you make it to be. Set your goal for a personal achievement. Give yourself a timeline. That creates motivation and determination. Measure your progress. Be encouraged, and when you achieve your objective, pat yourself on the back and give yourself a reward, because you have achieved success.

36

Ever Thought of Writing a Book?

I t is said that, "everyone has a book inside them." Whether that is true or not is debatable. What we do know is that everyone has a story to tell. Your life is a story unique to you. Most people enjoy stories. They enjoy the biographical bits and pieces of other people. It is not hard to readily identify with the joys, the struggles, and the ups and downs of other people's lives.

Have you ever thought of writing a book? Most people have at some point in their lives, whether it's to get your story out or just have your name on a book and feel a sense of accomplishment. I believe we all want to leave something behind to indicate we were here.

Do you have something to say? The vast majority of people would say no to that question – including me. However, it is rarely true. Once you begin the thought processes it will amaze you what comes to mind. In fact, you may find yourself in the same place where I know someone else is today. She began to write the story of her family. Sadly, she admits it is a somewhat dysfunctional family. Now 300 pages later she does not know when or where to finish. Life goes on with its twists and turns and while it does she continues to record it. I hope she will eventually conclude the story and find a readership for her probable 600-page book.

If you need to get yourself on the road to thinking of a subject to write about, then start with your life, your family, your upbringing, your schooling, your employment, your aspirations and desires, your career path, and all the other aspects that have given your life direction. Think about how you have interacted with people. What influences have certain people had upon you? Consider your reflections and memories that hold meaningful feelings.

My efforts began with wanting to share my early days with my children. Once my father had passed on I realized how little I knew about his background and upbringing, and now it was too late to ask. I determined that my children would not be in the same situation when I was not around. So I went back into my memory bank as far as possible and put down everything I could remember up to the time I got married—not that my life stopped there. It was just a convenient place to stop. I finished with 43 pages of happenings, events, and memories. The first 23 years of my life compressed into so few pages. Doesn't sound much but it brought some real satisfaction to hear the words from my children, "I didn't know about that in your life."

After having written this account of my early life, I realized there were events in my last twenty years before retirement that nobody knew about—family or others. The last twenty years of my working life were spent as executive director for a Christian mission working in Eastern Europe. This required travel into that part of the world. So for the sake of my family I started putting on paper the stories I could remember from that time. Those stories eventually formed the basis of my first book, published in 2009, entitled, *If We Only Knew*. It was then revised and republished in 2014 under the title of *Miracles: Coincidence or Divine Intervention?*

A while after the first book was out in the market place I began to wonder whether I could write another. I considered that, having been a public speaker for a number of years, I should be able to put something worthwhile on paper. If not, then had I even been saying anything worthwhile for those years? The end result was *Real Faith: What's at the Heart of the Gospel?* published in 2012.

You are now reading my third attempt. Maybe I am being influenced by Benjamin Franklin's words, "If you want to be remembered after you are dead, write something worth reading or do something worth writing." All of my book writing began after retirement. Today I do not write from the perspective that I know all the ropes, but only from the point of view that I would like to encourage all who would aspire to put pen to paper or perhaps all who should do that.

You may not want to write about yourself but another subject in which you have an interest. That's fine. What you need to do is to determine primarily what you want to say with your book. Set about doing an outline as to how best to present your case and finally do the proper research.

There are no hard and fast rules as to how long all these things should take. Your personal story all hinges on your memories. The timetable of your potential non-fiction book will depend upon the amount of research you need to do before you commit pen to paper. Fiction is a completely different ball game, about which I know very little to nothing. My own writing time was approximately one year researching and one year writing for each book. You might be much faster than I was but don't expect to write your book overnight—and have it a best seller.

To accomplish your objective of having a book in your hands and those of your friends, you will need to exercise incredible discipline. It is so easy to let other things crowd out your writing project. Try to write each day even if it is just a small amount. You will be surprised at your progress. You will begin by creating your first draft, then doing some rewriting and finally a serious edit—maybe by someone else. All of this is necessary to finish with a publishable manuscript and a book of which you will be proud.

Once completed, you will need to think about how it should be published. Most of us amateur writers think in terms of self-publishing, which has now become very acceptable in the publishing world. It is accessible, affordable, and convenient. It offers print-on-demand books, which means you can order a small number—even 5 copies if they are just for your family. Then if you are more serious you can have your book available as an e-book for Kindle and other Electronic readers. The doors are wide open to get your story to the waiting public.

After Words

We have talked about the body, the brain, the mind, and many other aspects of life that affect us in our everyday living. The following two chapters deal with two specific areas of life. The first is "Confessions of a Caregiver," in which I write from personal experience to encourage those who are currently taking care of a spouse or a parent, or are likely to in the future. The second is "View from the Pew," in which I dig a little into our spiritual side of life. It is simply my perspective on having a faith.

Depending upon your belief system, you may or may not want to read that chapter, and that is fine. It is your prerogative. Even for those who read it, I well understand that you may not agree with me or perhaps not agree on all issues. However, as I consider it an important aspect of life, I have included it. I believe it provides a balance when thinking about the body, soul, and spirit.

37

Confessions of a Caregiver

My wife, Rita, has had Parkinson's since 2008. Consequently, I have become a caregiver. I am not an expert, far from it, I am still learning, but let me share a few thoughts on being a caregiver in the hope that it might encourage you if you are in the same situation. Caregiving is not easy.

The simplest definition of caregiving is to provide physical and emotional support to those who are unable to care for themselves. But I believe it is more than that. I believe it is to create the very best environment and the best living conditions so that the person cared for enjoys life to the fullest possible extent, in spite of any incapacity.

The care we give develops and grows over time, from the normal assistance and help, to ultimately full time twenty-four-hour attention. One begins by doing simple things in the course of a regular day which help and provide support, but then as the incapacities grow so does the need for help. The person cared for slowly becomes incapable of doing most routine daily activities. To me that has been painful.

To see deterioration in the one you love is difficult to handle. One morning you wake up to realize that anything and everything that is to be done has to be done by you and that's not just for one day but from here on in, every day! That thought is daunting and disturbing.

If one is caring for a spouse, then it comes naturally out of the marriage relationship—it is all part of the commitment. Remember the wedding day and the words, "in sickness and in health." Never did we think it would apply like this. This is where reality sets in.

If you care for a parent, usually it is because you have accepted the responsibility, maybe because there is no one else to do the job. You recognized the need and have chosen to stand in the gap, strap on the load, and commit to being the child again, but this time the roles have reversed and the responsibility for care has fallen on your shoulders.

It may be difficult to imagine but caregiving is not all negative. It brings its own rewards. For the most part those cared for appreciate the assistance they receive and recognize the effort, and maybe the sacrifice, expended on their behalf. Deep gratitude is never far below the surface even if it is not always verbalized.

Is this caregiving a chore, a challenge, or a privilege? If we are honest it can be a chore. In fact, it is often hard work. It certainly is a challenge at times, but if you really love the person then it is a privilege. God has allowed me the privilege to care for my wife and therefore I do it to the very best of my ability.

UNDERSTANDING THE SITUATION

It is difficult to be of any use if we do not first learn to understand why we have to do what we do. Whether we are here by choice or not, the result is the same. We all deal with the same issues. We need to find out as much as we can to do the job as best we can. It may sound simple but it is critical to understand both sides of the coin.

We are on one side of the coin but your spouse or parent for whom you care is on the other side. Think about this. They didn't ask to be where they are. It certainly is not their fault that they now need care. They don't want to be in that condition. In fact, they don't like it. They probably hate it. They would rather be independent like everyone else.

How they would still love to dress themselves and cook the dinner. They would prefer to have the ability to do the laundry and iron the clothes, even if there were times earlier in life when those were not their most favorite tasks. Now they feel like a burden, a nuisance, an inconvenience to all around. If we are to comprehend their situation fully we need to get into their mind. We need to feel their sense of helplessness. The last thing they want is to be dependent upon others. They desperately need our kindness and understanding.

From our side, it is not uncommon to feel overwhelmed by taking on this task or having fallen into the task. But to do the job well we need to understand the tremendous needs on one side and our responsibility on the other. A good place to start is to get to know the disease you are dealing with. You cannot have too much knowledge as to how it might play out over the months and possibly years ahead. I read a 500-page book on Parkinson's, but that may seem a little over the top. It certainly helped me to understand the disease, what to expect, and what to look for.

By learning about the illness, you are not surprised along the way and accept what you see for what it is. You can also be an emotional support when the person cared for becomes disturbed by new symptoms. Find out what the medicine is supposed to be doing and how best it can and should be administered. The more you know about the disability the better you can handle it, because you can operate from a position of knowledge. It also helps your communication with medical personnel.

Take time to discover the physical and emotional suffering of the person receiving care. Listen intently to what they say and how they say it. Respect their thinking. It is they who are experiencing the disability. The more we know the more effective we will be in our caring.

What Is Required of Us?

Every situation is different and has its own unique challenges. Those who have to deal with dementia and Alzheimer's have their own set of hurdles. With Parkinson's I think the slowness and inability of movement, which every patient has to endure, is the cause of much frustration in both the caregiver and those cared for. Everything happens in slow motion. Anything that can still be done by the person themselves is painfully slow.

I remember the day when my wife said, "Hurry is no longer in my vocabulary." She was right. There is little point in saying, "Hurry up," because that adds frustration to the frustration. Allowing adequate time is the only solution. Leave extra preparation time. Adjust your thinking to accommodate delays. Something often goes wrong and at a time when you least need it to occur. Remember that frustration can easily lead to irritability, which is no help to anyone. We as caregivers are especially vulnerable to this when we feel unwell ourselves and we know that we still have to do all the tasks which only we can do.

The great danger with slowness is that the caregiver wants to jump in and do things because they know they can do them much faster. We have to resist that. We are there to help the cared for to be as independent as possible. It only makes them feel worse if small things which they can do are snatched away from them. As caregivers, we have to be willing to allow things to take place at a snail's pace. One has to remember that time is not of the essence in these circumstances but the emotional health of those cared for is. How much better for them to be praised for a small accomplishment than to be ready to go out of the house a couple of minutes earlier.

What do we need the most? A sense of humor goes a long way to keeping things on an even keel. Nobody wants to be laughed at but most enjoy being laughed with. There are funny sides to many of the issues we have to deal with. I think the sentence, "If you didn't laugh you would cry," probably has its place here.

The times I have put pants on back to front is hilarious. Learning to cook and do the meals was another laughable occupation. I graduated from a fried or boiled egg to something more substantial but not without mishaps on the way. So remember, laughter is important because it covers up awkwardness. It releases tension. It allows for joint acceptance of mistakes. A sense of humor will carry you through an otherwise tiresome day.

On a more serious note I would say we need love and patience. I think love must precede patience. When I say love I don't mean just a sense of pity, but loving the person for who they are and for who they have been and are to you at this moment. The situation calls for us to love them in it and through it.

We always need patience for the daily activities like the difficulty in dressing and the inability to cooperate, even if the desire to cooperate is there. Sensitivity and patience are especially called for when in public. Do the assisting as unobtrusively as possible, not making a show of it. It is natural that incapacities bring on self-consciousness and even embarrassment. In our public caring, we need to minimize and alleviate that as much as possible.

TAKE A BREAK!

Please don't think I am an expert at this. I am good at sharing more than I practice. I speak to myself on this issue as much as to others. My problem, maybe like you, is that I think I should be able to cope. When you feel healthy you imagine that you can do it but I am told it eventually catches up on you—with tiredness and exhaustion.

In the doctor's words to me, "You must take care of yourself, otherwise you will get sick and then who will do the caring?" Naturally she is right. So what do we do? What does respite mean? It means a change, a break, doing something other than the caring responsibilities. It means getting your mind on something else, maybe reading, playing a sport, or going to a concert. It could mean a change of venue to enjoy an evening of quietness and rejuvenation. I find writing to be a diversion and a respite.

My wife and I enjoy watching various sports and a few favorite television programs. This is relaxing in itself and at the same time I remain available if needed. I know it means remaining on call, but these are down times from the regular chores. It took me a long time to ask for help but I now arrange for visitors for my wife on evenings when I might need to go out. I understand that, if possible, there should also be days away. That is more difficult. I am told that a four-day break is as good as a three-week vacation. To get someone to help for a few hours is easier than a whole day. It is even more difficult to get someone for a few days' break, although I understand it is not impossible.

Intelligence reminds us that to do nothing will take its toll on our physical and emotional health. It is easy not to recognize the adverse effects it is having on our health. Others see what we cannot see in ourselves. A friend told me that he had no idea of how far down the hill his health had gone until he stopped his 24/7 care for his wife. If we ignore proper care of ourselves we are in danger of suffering from exhaustion, and ultimately burnout.

You may already have found yourself in a state of fatigue or regularly being tired from disturbed nights. The normal stress of life will always be with us but we must avoid abnormal and constant stress. It brings on long-term health problems. It has the ability to creep up on us and will then show itself in different ways. It can cause irrational or unwarranted anger or irritability. We can become overly anxious about mundane things and begin worrying about unrealistic things. We can feel down, sad, or worse, depressed. We can react unreasonably to minor issues. It is not uncommon to feel alone and isolated or to feel overwhelmed.

PRACTICAL SUGGESTIONS

Let's look at a few practical ways to help us cope. Make contingency plans for various scenarios. Involve your family in your plans. We are in a retirement community today because of discussions with our family. They have your best interest at heart. Make short term and long term plans. There has to be a balance between the needs of the cared for and the caregiver. Try to eat well and sleep well, neither of which is a guarantee.

It has taken a while but I have reached the point

where I try not to go beyond what I can reasonably carry out. If something is too much to handle, then I have to be willing to admit it. It is hard but we must not be afraid to ask for help both inside and outside the family. It may be surprising but there are folks who are just waiting to help.

Caregivers need support from others. It is good if you have a close trusted friend upon whom you can reflect or share feelings and concerns. There are caregiver groups which provide the mental and emotional support needed. That help brings confidence and assurance that we are not in this alone. I think I am learning a hard lesson, which is, we fail to ask for help to our peril.

When Does It All End?

Looking squarely at the future is difficult. There is no magic pill that makes all this go away. Hard as it is to say this, the task will get no easier than it is today. The demands will grow and the responsibilities will grow with them. Individual routine activities will become more difficult. However, the greater difficulty will be knowing when enough is enough and admitting the job is too much. Nobody wants that day to arrive.

I understand that most people go beyond their bearable level of total exhaustion. Pushed by the mindset of, "I should be able to do this," or, "Who else can do this but me?" we are tempted to continue doing what we do and maybe even to the detriment of those for whom we care. The progression of becoming totally exhausted is so slow that it is virtually impossible to recognize. It is not until we find ourselves constantly tired and falling asleep every time we sit down that we might begin to admit that the job just might be getting too much. The justifiable fear is what happens beyond that. None of us wants to go there—well I certainly don't.

I guess this is where the long-term planning I mentioned earlier comes into play. This is where we recall the discussion with other family members, and consider all options for everyone involved. Usually there is the option of hiring assistance from outside, which would be considered assisted living. Beyond that it would have to be long-term care. This would be a very hard scenario. It is disturbing and hurts just to think about that possibility.

This is a personal view and you might think differently, but I believe my Christian faith certainly helps in facing all of these issues both now and in the future. I would be the first to acknowledge that there are thousands upon thousands of people doing an admirable job at caregiving who would not profess to have any kind of faith. So, having a faith is not a pre-requisite or essential for caregiving. I can speak only from my own experience and I believe my faith provides support in my role as caregiver.

As a source of strength—not physical but spiritual— I believe it helps me face the difficulties and disappointments of everyday caregiving. It doesn't change the situation or make things any less painful but it does seem to provide the strength to overcome and rise above an unenviable situation. Knowing that God cares brings consolation and comfort. From this comes an inner peace and inexplicable strength. Believing that we are in God's hands gives confidence that whatever is in the present and whatever lies before us will be His concern as well. With that in mind I press on to do my caregiving to the best of my ability; that's what I have chosen to do.

So my fellow Caregivers, keep working, keep helping, keep loving, and be encouraged. Even if not expressed, your efforts are deeply appreciated. You are important because you play an important role. In fact, you are indispensable. You are the pillar that provides critical support. One day you will have a sense of comfort and satisfaction in the knowledge that you did the best you could. That is all anyone can expect of you.

38

A View from the Pew

In times past we might have expected "fire and brimstone" sermons from the pulpit. Today we receive reasoned presentations of Christian faith principles, how they work, and how they should work out in our lives. I would like briefly to share some of those principles which form the basis of the Christian Faith.

We are all believers. By that I mean that we all have a belief system. The atheist believes there is no God. The agnostic is not sure whether there is a God or not, whereas the Christian wholeheartedly believes in God. Whatever it is we believe forms the basis for our actions.

THE EXISTENCE OF GOD

All belief has a foundation. The Christian faith has a two-fold foundation, the existence of God and the Bible. This is the question that humanity has wrestled with since the beginning of time. The mystery of God's existence has occupied the minds of philosophers and scientists for centuries. In fact, it has been said that this is probably the greatest and most important question that anyone can ask. Our answer is crucial because it forms the basis upon which we build our whole belief system.

Some might ask, "How can one believe in God without outward physical evidence?" It is true that we cannot see God, but we are not without outward evidence. No one would dispute the existence of the wind after a tornado has passed through a town. We cannot see it yet we believe in its existence. No one disputes the existence of gravity when they see the result of a rock-slide or a man falling from a scaffold. The evidence is indisputable. Yet we cannot see gravity. Thus it is with God. We may not be able to see him with our eyes but we have the Bible, the world, and life itself, which give us conclusive evidence of his existence.

For the Christian, that God exists is an indisputable fact, supported by the overwhelming evidence given in creation, in nature, in science, and in astronomy. Scores of books have been written confirming the unique and exquisite design of the universe and the delicate balance within the order of creation. We learn that the world has been perfectly placed in the universe to create an environment to sustain life on earth. Even secular astronomers and scientists are admitting to an intelligent design within the universe and are almost embarrassingly faced with the evidence of a Creator.

Hugh Ross in his book *The Creator of the Cosmos* quotes Allan Sandage, a winner of the Crafoord Prize in astronomy (equivalent to the Nobel Prize) who, while not acknowledging to be a man of faith, remarked, "I find it quite improbable that such order came out of chaos.

There has to be some organizing principle. God to me is a mystery but it is the explanation for the miracle of existence, why there is something instead of nothing." God has revealed himself, and goes on revealing himself.

In his book *In Understanding Be Men*, T. C. Hammond states, "There is a world-wide intuition in the heart of man that there is a Supreme Being who is to be worshipped. Although this intuition expresses itself in very many different ways .... Its existence provides strong evidence of the existence of God." He goes on to say that, "...the existence of God is fundamental to our thinking." The understanding of humanity and life itself hinges upon our acceptance of the existence of God. Without God, life would not fit together. Without God, life would be an unsolvable puzzle. Without God, we would not exist.

If the magnificence of the universe does not provide enough evidence of God's existence, then perhaps we should consider the complexity of the human body. The smallest cell among the trillions in the body stores a mind-boggling amount of information, yet everything fits together and operates the whole like a well-oiled machine. The brain alone is so intricately constructed and functions with infinitesimal accuracy that it supersedes all human-created computers.

The truth of God's existence is not dependent upon our knowledge or acceptance of the facts presented. We all have the right to choose whether to believe it or not. My personal view is that we ignore the evidence to our detriment. It was Bishop Robinson from London,

England, who in the early sixties declared "God is dead!" I sometimes wondered what else he would have to say to his parishioners as a Bishop after that statement. However, the outcome of his declaration is this. Bishop Robinson is now dead and God is still very much alive!

The Bible

Most religions are based upon the teachings of a man, or a prophet, a spiritual guru, or a set of spiritual or philosophical principles. The basis and authority of the Christian faith is unique because its basis is twofold, the teaching of Jesus and the Holy Scriptures. It is true that the Bible was the work of humans. In fact, about 40 men wrote from their different backgrounds and experiences, but they wrote under the inspiration of the Holy Spirit. What does that mean? It was not dictation, but their writing was certainly inspired, guided and orchestrated by the work of God's Spirit, although each man's personality can be seen within their writings. When you see the order, the harmony, and the coordination throughout Scripture, penned by so many different writers over hundreds of years, it leaves little doubt that humans could not have achieved this on their own.

Through the prophecies of the Old Testament the authors foretold hundreds of events which were to take place almost a thousand years later. The New Testament records the fulfillment of those prophecies down to extraordinary detail. We see this particularly in the birth, the life, the ministry, the death, and the resurrection of Jesus.

The Bible has proved its authenticity many times over. It has been confirmed historically, geographically, archeologically, prophetically and, of course, spiritually. It is now thought that most of the books of the New Testament were written no later than 80 AD. That is less than fifty years from the death of Christ; and with the existence today of at least 24,000 total or partial manuscripts of the New Testament, this is ample literary proof of its authenticity. Few, if any, manuscripts in the literary world from Homer to Shakespeare can compare with such a record.

THE GOSPEL

So what is the message of the Bible and how does it apply to us in the 21st century? There is a thread running throughout Scripture that is God's message to the world. It is called the gospel. The word *gospel* means good news. The good news is that we can experience the love of God, receive forgiveness from Him, and enter into a personal relationship with Him through Jesus Christ. This is a simplified version of the gospel in non-theological terms. Some may need to forgive me for offering so simple an explanation. For those who desire to read a more in-depth presentation, there are plenty of other resources to provide just that.

So why do we need forgiveness? Because we have an inherent propensity to do wrong. Do you have to teach children to misbehave? According to the Bible that wrongdoing is classified as sin and while it remains unresolved in our lives it hinders any relationship with God because God is holy, and holiness and sin cannot mix. Hence there is a gap or break in our relationship with God which can only be corrected through forgiveness. All forgiveness comes at a price. A conflict between two people is put right only by one paying a price. One admits the wrong, expresses remorse, and seeks forgiveness.

Forgiveness between people can be resolved by a little humility, a little remorse, and things can be set right, but there is nothing that we can do to right the situation with God. We cannot buy our forgiveness by doing good works. There is no price we could pay God to receive His forgiveness. However, God, in his love, stepped in and paid the price for our forgiveness by giving his son Jesus Christ to die on the cross. Without that forgiveness we are condemned to a place of isolation from the presence of God. Christ removed that condemnation by his death on the cross. It's interesting that Jesus said, "I am the Way, the Truth and the Life." Thus he indicates he did not come just to preach about the truth but he was the Truth, He was the message. This is confirmed by his death and resurrection.

The purpose of the gospel is simply that men and women can have a personal relationship with Jesus Christ. God freely offers the gift of salvation but does not force us to accept the gift. The Christian faith calls for a personal response. There is no such thing as a secondhand faith. One cannot be grandfathered in by parental faith or by being a member of a church or part of any religious group. People decide individually to accept the Christian faith.

A one sentence outline of the gospel is this: God is holy, humanity is sinful, and the only way they can be brought together is through the plan instigated by God and carried out through the person and work of Jesus Christ. In other words, God loves us and offers us forgiveness through his son Jesus Christ and an on-going life-long relationship with him. The Christian faith is not a matter of worshipping a distant, unknown divine Being, but a close walk with God who is ever present with the believer.

Blaise Pascal, a seventeenth-century philosopher, suggested that, "...there is a God-shaped vacuum within the heart of man." If that is so, then we will search forever until a relationship has been established with God.

A FOLLOWER OF CHRIST

What then is a true Christian? Is it someone who just does what he thinks is right? Is it someone who is obviously good and caring? Is it someone who expresses concern for others and goes out of his or her way to help alleviate pain and suffering? Is that the essence of a true Christian? These certainly display Christian traits. However, people do not necessarily have to be a Christian to perform such acts of kindness. Some who have no religious affiliation at all do good things and make a difference to the lives of others and their community. But Christianity is more than just doing good deeds. You could be an atheist and still help your neighbor.

The true Christian is the person whose belief system

is based upon the Bible. This is the authority outside of him or herself. This is the foundation upon which the Christian faith is built. The teachings of Christ and the message of the gospel form the basis for faith. Once the gospel is accepted and a commitment made to become a follower of Christ, the person can then be called Christian. The Bible becomes the standard, the guide, the rule book by which the believer lives. The Christian should live out his or her life demonstrating the characteristics of Christ. That amounts to living a life of love, care, and concern for others.

The Bible also provides hope, assurance, and a confidence that God is in control regardless of circumstances. Thus, when life brings the adverse ups and downs, the Christian, although maybe still hurt and suffering like others, enjoys a peace which comes from God himself. True Christians are unperturbed by the brickbats thrown their way by an opposing world because the foundation of trust and faith is found in Jesus Christ alone.

Some people dislike the words *Christian conversion*. The word *conversion* is commonplace. It just conveys the aspect of change. The word is used in most religions and even in a secular and practical sense when a building is converted to a secondary use. So in our context we ask the question, "Is Christian conversion really necessary?" To which the answer is, "Only if you want to become a follower of Christ."

Referenced Books

Chapter 7. *Chasing Daylight: How My Forthcoming Death Transformed My Life*, by Eugene O'Kelly. Published by McGraw-Hill.

Chapter 10. *In Praise of Slow: How a Worldwide Movement Is Challenging the Cult of Speed*, by Carl Honoré. Published by Vintage Canada.

Chapter 12. *Mindfulness*, by Ellen J. Langer. Published by Da Capo Press.

Chapter 13. *Why the Universe Is the Way It Is*, by Hugh Ross. Published by Baker Books.

Chapter 17. *The Man Who Touched His Own Heart: True Tales of Science, Surgery, and Mystery*, by Rob Dunn. Published by Little Brown and Company.

Chapter 23. *Loneliness*, by John Cacioppo and William Patrick. Published by W. W. Norton & Company.

Chapter 24. *None of These Diseases: The Bible's Health Secrets for the 21st Century*, by Dr. S. I. McMillen. Published by Spire Books.

Chapter 34. *Switch On Your Brain: The Key to Peak Happiness, Thinking, and Health*, by Dr. Caroline Leaf. Published by Baker Books.

Chapter 38. *The Creator and the Cosmos: How the Latest Scientific Discoveries Reveal God*, by Hugh Ross. Published by Navpress.

In Understanding Be Men: An Introductory Handbook on Christian Doctrine, by T.C.Hammond. Published by Inter-Varsity Fellowship.

Other books by John Murray

Miracles: Coincidence or Divine Intervention?

Real Faith: What's at the Heart of the Gospel?

Information on these books is available at
www.jmurray.ca

To connect with the author:

email: murray150@fastmail.fm
website: www.jmurray.ca
twitter: @AuthorJMurray
facebook.com/AuthorJohnMurray